To Bran
from
Olivia

Black Youth in Crisis

Black Youth in Crisis

edited by
Ernest Cashmore
Department of Sociology and Social History
The University of Aston in Birmingham
and

Barry Troyna
SSRC Research Unit on Ethnic Relations
The University of Aston in Birmingham

London
GEORGE ALLEN & UNWIN
Boston   Sydney

George Allen & Unwin (Publishers) Ltd,
40 Museum Street, London WC1A 1LU, UK

George Allen & Unwin (Publishers) Ltd,
Park Lane, Hemel Hempstead, Herts HP2 4TE, UK

Allen & Unwin, Inc.,
9 Winchester Terrace, Winchester, Mass. 01890, USA

George Allen & Unwin Australia Pty Ltd,
8 Napier Street, North Sydney, NSW 2060, Australia

First published in 1982

British Library Cataloguing in Publication Data

Black youth in crisis.
    1. Minority youth–Great Britain–Socioeconomic status
I. Cashmore, Ernest   II. Troyna, Barry
305.8'00941   JA125.A1
ISBN 0-04-362052-3
ISBN 0-04-362053-1 Pbk

Library of Congress Cataloging in Publication Data

   Main entry under title:
   Black youth in crisis.
Bibliography: p.
Includes index.
1. Youth, Black—Great Britain—Attitudes—Addresses, essays,
lectures.   2. Great Britain—Social conditions—1945–   —Addresses,
essays, lectures.   3. Great Britain—Economic conditions—1945–
—Addresses, essays, lectures.   4. Great Britain—Race
relations—Addresses, essays, lectures.   I. Cashmore, Ernest.   II.
Troyna, Barry.
DA125.N4B53   1982   305.8'96'041   82-11402
ISBN 0-04-362052-3 (papercased)
ISBN 0-04-362053-1 (pbk.)

Set in 10 on 11 point Century Schoolbook by
Computape (Pickering) Ltd, North Yorkshire
and printed in Great Britain by
Biddles Ltd, Guildford, Surrey

Contents

Black Youth in Crisis

Introduction

Black youth in Britain is changing dramatically. The ferocity of purpose young blacks recently brought to their challenges at St Paul's in Bristol, Handsworth in Birmingham, Highfields in Leicester and Brixton in London, indicates not merely dissatisfaction with social conditions or disillusionment with their own positions, but a new destructive energy, an undisciplined enthusiasm for confrontation. The change in orientation is not new, nor has it been indiscernible; but it has been gestating for the last few years. Intermittent disorders at the Notting Hill carnivals and at Wolverhampton in the West Midlands (in 1978) were dispersed and then neutralised as not being racially based. But, as *New Society* (10 April 1980) pointed out, the establishment reaction to such occurrences revolves around 'the inability to see racism as a distinct variable in community relations' and this reveals 'a depressing inability to cope with an issue' which is not so much emergent as imminent.

The well-publicised 'riots' of Bristol and Brixton, and the lesser-known incidents of Handsworth and Highfields were localised and containable. Yet they articulated genuine protests against the actions of whites generally, and the police in particular; and the outcomes of such episodes can do nothing to improve already rapidly deteriorating relationships. The unsettling aspect of it all is that black youths are vigorously contributing to the deterioration; many are consciously trying to break down what they regard as an inappropriate dependence on white society.

Young blacks in the main, whether West Indian or of West Indian descent, have been depicted as the recipients of 'pressure': restricted employment opportunities, police discrimination, bad inner-city accommodation, inadequate education, the whole cluster of forces emanating from white racialism. It is a familiar role for them; the episodes of early 1980 give fresh clues as to an alternative. There is a much more active part for the black youth to play now that the pattern has begun to form; and the possibility must now be faced that a sequence of events resembling Bristol and Brixton may spiral into an ugly complex of unrest and disorder.

The Bristol occurrence was generously covered by the media, but further perspective can be gained from events which followed it in Birmingham and Leicester on 5 May and 28 July 1980 respectively. In Birmingham, the affair started after a break-in at a store. The intruders were described to the police by the proprietor, and two patrolling police officers acted on the description and apprehended two black youths who were, it seems, known to them. Strong resistance was offered by the youths who were assisted by some other young blacks in beating up the police officers (one suffered a broken collar-bone and smashed ribs). The affray attracted the attention of passers-by, one of whom alerted nearby Thornhill Road police station. When police arrived to rescue the distraught officers, they were met by a hail of bricks and their presence stimulated more violence. The two policemen were eventually recovered, both unconscious.

Because they were known to the police, the suspected youths were traced to an address from where they were later picked up and taken to Thornhill Road police station. What followed was one of the most striking scenes of collective black endeavour in Handsworth since the National Front rally of 1977. An estimated two hundred black youths congregated at the police station and demanded the release of the two. The reception area filled and threats multiplied as the station was besieged. An additional seventy police officers were recruited from surrounding areas. Negotiations were hastily conducted between spontaneously appointed black spokesmen and the station's senior police officer. The crowd was eventually dispersed and order was restored: the two young blacks were granted bail.

The episode did not escalate into anything like the Bristol proportions, but it had similar ingredients nevertheless: the precipitating assault on the police officers after the apprehension of the two black youths under suspicion; the effective mobilisation of some two hundred black youths in reaction to the perceived injustice; the willingness of the police to compromise (as they did in a different way in Bristol) when faced with what was obviously a forceful threat; and crucially, the blacks' perception of their own effectiveness in imposing their wishes on a collective basis. They did get something done; a tangible result was achieved which would not have been possible had they approached the matter in a less direct way.

In one sense, the issue is disappointing for the Handsworth community whose police force had prided itself on a steady improvement in its relations with black youth since the beginning of 1978 when foot-patrol officers were reintroduced in a creditable attempt to cultivate personal links with the rest of the multi-ethnic community. The changes in policing were made after the publication of the notorious and distorted *Shades of Grey* (1977) report which presented an apocalyptic vision of the area poised on the brink of unrest – what one provincial newspaper, in a review of the report, called 'a powder keg situation' (*Birmingham Evening Mail*, 6 December 1977).

The over-representation of blacks in crimes relating to assaults and other street crimes subsided and signs were generally promising. The Thornhill Road episode was particularly damaging.

The change in policing policy in the direction of more community involvement was well intentioned and certainly did no harm; but those who chose to see it as a solution tended to misunderstand the nature of the problem which is rooted in the ghetto with its perplexing and obstructing disunities – in particular, one section of the ghetto occupied by young blacks. This group has made it quite clear that it does not intend to succumb to any attempt to integrate it into the mainstream of the society. Black youths are in the process of cultivating their own distinct values, interests, meanings and ambitions; they reject efforts to resolve their problems as inapposite. Accounts of their dishonesty and arrogance are not uncommon and they themselves do nothing to suggest that the accounts are inaccurate. Thus follows the possibility that when such a problem becomes recalcitrant, we ignore it; the feeling amongst young blacks is that they want to be left to such devices.

This was underlined by the episode, again involving black youth and the police, in the Highfields district of Leicester in July 1980. Here, the apprehension of a young Rasta on a suspicion of malicious damage – an unmarked police car parked outside a pub frequented by young blacks, had had its windows smashed and body scratched – sparked off a series of violent confrontations between black youth and the police which lasted most of the night. Again, the retaliatory action of the young blacks to this arrest was on a collective basis and its impact is still reverberating not only in Highfields but in the chambers of Leicester City Council. On the one hand, black youth now stubbornly resist any conciliatory moves by the police and, as attitudes towards one another have become even more firmly entrenched, relations between the police and the black community in this district, and beyond, have reached a low ebb. On the other hand, the collective resistance to the police that night has produced an immediate response from the city council and plans are now underway to provide the population in Highfields with much-needed community, educational and recreational resources and services. What happened that night is important for other reasons. First, because it showed for the first time that black youth in Highfields were able and prepared to mobilise in response to perceived discriminatory police practices. Secondly, it added further credence to the view that the image of Leicester as 'a shining example of how successful a multi-racial society can be' (Edward Heath, pre-general election speech, Leicester, April 1979) is largely illusory (see also Troyna, 1981). The parallels with Bristol are self-evident.

The complex of problems connected with black youth is compounded by every successive round of unqualified school-leavers recruited to the lower orders of the occupational world or registered with the Department of Employment. The 'twilight activities' of thieving and hustling are seen by some as 'strategies of survival', almost inevitable alternatives to mainstream existences. Many young blacks are resisting attempts to negotiate or compromise. Youth in the ghetto are feeling different: they have their own antagonistic values, and frequently oppositional attitudes.

If nothing else, the episodes at St Paul's, Handsworth and Highfields taught young blacks one thing: they can collectively produce results, if only in the short term. The sheer potential of undisciplined violence got them results, possibly not significant in overall terms and productive of no palpable improvement. But they saw the episode as socially meaningful happenings: they showed themselves and each other what they can do when their concerns crystallise around specific issues. Solid phalanxes of young blacks can be influential even if they lack a real direction. The potential to disrupt is enormous and the fact that black youth now realises this was attested to by the most dramatic uprising to date, in Brixton in April 1981.

The recent instances may well presage a new response of hostility from young blacks; and what makes the prospect less pleasant is the fact that there are few measures with which to confront the response, save for the tightening of social control which, while a grim possibility, can only suppress, and will certainly not solve, the problem.

The legal measures implemented in the 1960s were meant to obviate the type of problems thrown up by black dissidence in the USA, but the ineffectiveness of such procedures is now clear. Only some massive transformation of attitudes and postures towards black youth and, critically, on their behalf, can ameliorate the problem and this Laputan ideal is no realistic solution. The problem has been wrought out of years of relegating blacks to inferior statuses and exposing their sons and daughters to this fact whilst offering them no alternative to organise their lives around. The second generation perceive clearly that blackness is a potential obstacle to advancement in society and its members have now resigned themselves to this perception. They cannot delude themselves and so have cultivated values and attitudes which elevate that quality of blackness to a position of importance. For many young blacks, being black is the salient link which unites them in the face of what they regard as an unaccommodating society.

There is little scope for optimism in this appraisal. There are no signs of improvement and, ignoring for the moment Driver's questionable findings (1980), the general situation at school level augurs badly for the future. The school produces black incumbents of lower-grade jobs or unemployment queues. The situation is acute and a significant number of black youth are emotionally prepared for violence as a strategy or attempted solution. However unwilling we may be to accept it, the episodes of the first few months of the decade may be the first meaningful clues as to the responses young blacks will increasingly opt for in the future.

This was the disturbing prospect before us when we set forth to compile this collection of readings organised around the theme of black youth. We were also aware that we might not be able to offer any optimistic, meaningful alternatives to this prospect. In the event, we are not, and we elaborate upon the reason for this in Chapter 2. 'Crisis' is a key word here: it is a crisis carved out of a combination of material circumstances and perceptions of reality.

The transition from school to work (or the dole queues) we see as of pivotal importance in the production of crisis. Many young blacks are convinced of the uselessness of curricula in terms of their present and future lives. Why? This we also attempt to unravel in Chapter 2. Is the content and structure of education in Britain balanced against black youth? If not, why do they react against it or just demonstrate apathy towards it?

One of the results of these orientations of black youth to education is that they are ill-prepared for work. They understand themselves to be funnelled into unproductive and uncreative work; they have few alternatives to the traditional roles handed down by their parents.

In fact, as we write, it becomes increasingly evident that even these traditional roles may not be available at all. Unemployment is affecting black youth disproportionately. Thus:

> Between November 1973 and November 1977, while national unemployment figures doubled, unemployment figures among ethnic minorities quadrupled (PEP). This trend is continuing. According to DE statistics, from February 1979 to February 1980, ethnic minority unemployment has risen four times as fast as overall unemployment.
>
> By May 1980, the increase in ethnic minorities' unemployment for the previous twelve months had reached 25·8 per cent.
>
> The overall change among the unemployed aged under 18 in Britain for the twelve months to January 1980 was a *reduction* of 2·4 per cent;

the increase among ethnic minorities was 7·3 per cent. (Commission for Racial Equality, 1980, pp. 13–14)

But unemployment is not a cause of the problems surrounding young blacks: it exacerbates them. We must look deeper.

The economic cutbacks of the 1970s and 1980s do not help. Resources are less available to the community generally, and to schools in particular. But were the projects these resources were available for effective in the first place? Over ten years of urban aid grants, community development projects and education priority area programmes has had a questionable input – particularly on black youth. State aid is not the final answer: the problems are more entrenched in the furrows of culture, power and identity. Poverty, alone, is an inadequate explanation of the kinds of scenes witnessed in the early 1980s.

These are the kinds of areas we attempt to analyse in the chapters that follow. We have put together a collection of essays by people who, we realise, do not face these problems but are acutely aware of them. Because it is a book about black youth and not by black youth we realise that its worth may be questioned; certainly, in view of the negative conclusions that we reach. The practical and moral difficulties associated with the whole project, therefore, are made clear in Chapter 1.

A recurrent theme of the book is the theoretical and empirical inadequacy of 'black youth' as a discrete social category. As Sheila Allen comments in Chapter 9, black youth is a construction which 'oversimplifies the structure of a class society and the relations ... between classes, generations, genders and ethnic groups'. Moreover, it is clear from the extant literature that 'black youth' has become synonymous with young black males of West Indian descent. In this sense, then, those studies which have focused on the experiential world of young blacks have provided us with a partial view of that reality. Studies of 'black youth' can therefore be accused of reproducing the 'gaps' and 'distortions' which are characteristic of youth culture studies in general; only recently, for instance, have female youth cultures in and out of school begun to attract the attentions of social researchers (for example, McRobbie and Garber, 1976; Deem, 1980; Jones, 1980; Llewellyn, 1980). Mary Fuller's essay on a discernible subculture of young black girls in a London comprehensive school is therefore an important and necessary contribution (see Chapter 6). In this chapter, Fuller analyses the ways in which this small group of girls manifest their resistance to racism and the extent to which this differs from that of their male counterparts. She also points to the interaction of racism and sexism in contemporary

Britain and its impact on these girls' perception of their 'own sense of worth'.

Another prevalent characteristic of youth cultural analyses is the celebration of the 'deviant' or 'ecstatic' lifestyle of the young blacks. This, too, has been faithfully reproduced in empirically based studies of black youth; witness the overwhelming emphasis on their involvement in the Rastafarian movement. Of course, as John Rex indicates in Chapter 4, 'the drama of Rasta' is meaningful to all young West Indians and for this reason we have decided to include a chapter based on our own independent research on the progressive drift of black youth into Rasta ways (see Chapter 5). We see this drift as having its genesis not in the post-school experiences, as some commentators have insisted, but in the later stages of their secondary-school education. None the less, whilst including a chapter in the collection, we would fully endorse John Rex's statement that, although the commitment to a Rastafarian lifestyle is all too often taken to be 'the sole or typical representative of "immigrant" or "black" youth', 'there are a great many other possible immigrant situations'. All too often, however, black youths are perceived and defined as constituting a culture of resistance and this has had important implications for the way in which social policy towards this (heterogeneous) group of youngsters has been conceptualised and implemented. The contributions by Malcom Cross (Chapter 3) and George Fisher and Harry Joshua (Chapter 8) highlight the extent to which these policies have been initiated on false and misleading assumptions. Cross argues, for instance, that in various ways the marginality that black youth experience in this country can be seen as 'manufactured' by the social policies that have been advanced to cope with the presenting problems as they have been comprehended. Drawing on archival material relating to the West Indies, and published and unpublished data collected in Britain, Cross also argues that the British approach to black youth can be seen as an extension of colonial attitudes and assumptions.

The construction of 'black youth' as a social category also suggests, at least implicitly, that there is a disjunction not only between them and young whites but also between young blacks and their parents. The structural schism which is assumed to exist between black migrants and their British-born children is challenged in the chapters of Sheila Allen, and Fisher and Joshua. Allen rightly points to the scarcity of empirical evidence which would support the popularly conceived notion of these migrants as 'quiescent', 'conformist' and 'prepared to accept their lot'. The paucity of research-based evidence of the lives and experiences of the black migrants who arrived in Britain in the

1950s and 1960s is an important caveat when we come to assess the similarities and differences between their perceptions of life in Britain and those of their children. As Allen reminds us: 'When analysing the contemporary situation we have to acknowledge that many questions remain open and to close them by stereotypical portrayals of the older generation is a denial of generational experience and produces an impoverished analysis.'

Fisher and Joshua are sceptical of intergenerational dissension and conflict for other reasons. After all, they write, the growing number of young blacks 'positively involved in both re-articulating and extending radical, though increasingly central, aspects of the indigenous home culture' – principally via their commitment to the Rasta movement – can be regarded as a denial and contradiction of the assumption that these same black youths are estranged from their parents' generation, culture and homeland. Indeed, this takes on greater irony because affiliation to Rasta and reggae music (both generated in the parental homeland) is often interpreted by commentators as one of the main ways in which black youth publicly signify their detachment from, and rejection of, parental values and culture.

The pertinence and veracity of these critiques of 'black youth' does not, of course, deny that black youngsters encounter problems which are generated specifically by the way their blackness is defined in the wider society. Of these, it could be contended that the 1824 Vagrancy Act ('sus') is the most iniquitous. Brian Roberts argues in Chapter 7 that the significance of 'sus' extends to the wider discussion of police powers and practices and, in turn, to questions of civil rights and criminal procedure. More pertinent to the present volume, however, is the contention that the administration of the Act has created irreparable damage to the relationship between the police and black youth. Robert's detailed documentation of the evidence leads him to conclude: 'Not only has the use of the charge itself by the police created bitterness and resentment but also the issue has become a symbolic precis of the accumulation of the wide-ranging and serious criticisms that have been made against the police by the black community in recent years.' So, whilst there were sighs of relief when the Act was repealed during the 1980–1 parliamentary session, there were also fears that this decision had come far too late to effect any change in the black community's prevailing perception of the British police.

It seems almost platitudinous to end by saying that 'more research is needed'; however, the contributions by John Rex and Sheila Allen provide fruitful and productive avenues for future work. Both agree, for instance, that many of the existing contributions to the study of youth cultures (black and white) are imbalanced. John Rex's argument for more detailed ethnographic studies of black youth appears to be the most necessary and productive formulation for future studies. As he says, the research perspectives outlined in his chapter point 'not towards simple cross-tabulations of life-chances and social conditions so dearly loved by British empirical sociology, but to the collection of structured life histories to see how far these ideal types or stereotypes actually reflect the range of empirical reality'. Finally, in the concluding chapter, Sheila Allen alerts us once again to the scarcity of material relating to the experiences of black girls in Britain and suggests, amongst other things, that these experiences be 'made visible'. Only by documenting the ways in which the structuring of racism affects young black women, as well as their male counterparts, will we be in a position to develop a much richer understanding of 'black youth'.

The objective of this book, then, is not only to pose new questions about young blacks but to answer many of the existing ones in the light of new evidence and fresh theories: to place the issues in a new perspective. Our view that there is an imminent crisis constitutes an organising theme for the book and is also the reason for its existence in the first place. Much of what follows will not please those committed to integration and the formal methods available for achieving it. We write of the world as we see it and we make no apologies for our conclusions. We only hope that by opening up the very urgent possibilities of the future we may, in some measure, make them less probable.

Ernest Cashmore
Barry Troyna

1 Black Youth for Whites

ERNEST CASHMORE

One evening in late 1980, I watched a game of amateur soccer under the floodlights of an Islington stadium. With me stood a Jamaican-born man in his mid-20s who had been educated up to the age of 9 in Jamaica before moving to Leeds and then London. I had been introduced to him by one of the football team's captains as 'Ernest Cashmore – he's down here doing a project on black sportsmen and he's speaking to us, getting to know what we're about. I'll leave him with you.'

For ninety-odd minutes I chatted with Sydney Grant about football, about universities, about black people, about whites – and many more things. We exchanged opinions frankly and, for my part at least, without inhibition. I told him that I worked at the University of Aston and had previously been at the London School of Economics where I had done research on the Rasta-farian movement.

'Why?' he asked me.

'Well, I have an intrinsic interest to begin with', I answered. 'I was brought up in Handsworth and so am very aware of the situations and problems of living in such an area. I know a lot of black guys and like to think that I'm sensitive to the kinds of difficulties they face.' I could remember answering similar types of question in exactly the same fashion many times before. 'On top of that, I have a commitment to the improvement of race relations and I feel that the only way to move away from what must be a deteriorating situation is by understanding the views, experiences, problems of other groups. The Rastas were one such case.'

Grant kept his gaze fixed on the match, clearly unimpressed by my reasons. 'Tell me, who did you write it for?'

Wat had started as an interview of sorts in which I was supposed to be getting information about him was developing into an intellectual inquisition. I drew breath impatiently and replied: 'Well, I didn't particularly have an audience in mind when I began the project and, when the book came out, I still had ambitions that it would be read by as wide a span of people as possible; not just other academics or social workers, etc., but every-day guys who are seriously interested in the race-relations scene.'

'You mean whites?'

'No. I mean anybody who's interested; blacks as well as whites.'

'But you *are* writing for whites,' he insisted.

Once more I countered: 'Why should you think that? What makes you think that there aren't any blacks who are concerned about these types of issues and want to commit themselves?'

'There are', he answered. 'But they know what it's all about already without reading your book. They know 'cause they're black and know what it's like to live as a black person. You don't, so what can you tell them? *You're writing for whites.*'

When Barry Troyna and I got together to plan this book, we were both 'veterans' of one major piece of research on race-relations issues apiece. Not many months had passed since I had completed my work on the Rastafarian movement in England and Troyna his on the impact of reggae on the identities of young blacks in London and Midland schools. In our own ways, we felt that we had made finite, but hopefully valuable, contributions to the appreciation of blacks and, therefore, to the improvement of black–white relations. The conviction with which we made the link between the two was to be shaken.

At the time, we were both self-assured and confident enough to approach people whom we regarded as the foremost, distinguished commentators on black youth.

Our publishers endorsed the proposals and we proceeded to write, compile and edit a book which we felt would be the definitive work on young blacks in Britain in the late 1970s/early 1980s.

With our research backgrounds, we thought our ambitions were not extravagant, though not, of course, ultimately unchallengeable. 'Cocky', was how I was described by one reviewer of my book on the Rastas!

Throughout the initial period of assembling the chapters, neither Troyna nor myself ever questioned the validity of our enterprise. We strained to encompass perspectives by incorporating the views of people whom we felt to be, if not hostile, suspicious of such a venture (see Chapter 9). Independently, we moved in different research directions: Troyna on how the media structure perceptions of the National Front, and myself on why blacks get involved in sport and what social effects this will have. Neither of us felt insecure about our projects. We worked in the same orbit, sharing similar commitments and, we understood, holding the same sets of values (see Cashmore and Troyna, 1981).

The rationale behind our work, generally, and the *Black Youth* project, in particular, was an attempt to broaden understanding.

Concealment has never been one of my vices. When I began establishing contacts with Rastas in early 1977, I disclosed myself as a student from the LSE doing research on the movement with the intention of understanding the movement 'from the inside'. For the most part, the words reached receptive ears. After all, the movement had been given a toughish time by the media. One provincial paper had labelled it a 'mafia-style' organisation dealing in prostitution and dope, others had depicted it as a black power party or a 'lost tribe on the warpath'. The writers behind such stories had no doubt extracted their copy with the use of such questions as: 'What are the main beliefs of the movement?' 'Are you religious or political?' 'When did you become a Rasta?'

My approach was different: I encouraged Rastas to talk about things they were interested in and always tried to trade with them on level terms, offering my often contradictory opinions, but never condescending. The method produced bewilderment and perplexity at first, but the end-product was, I am led to believe – by Rastas – more satisfying than a great deal of other works. I offered neither conclusions, nor recommendations. My job, as I saw it, was to present the results as a way of understanding and letting the reader decide. I now believe that this was naïve, but have yet to come up with a solid alternative.

Whilst engaged on the black sportsmen project, I was asked by a white boxing coach whether I thought I could really get anything out of blacks which would tell us something new. He argued, very plausibly: 'No matter what you try to do, you're always talking *at* them.'

I disagreed, at first, and he went on: 'When all's said and done, you're white, you're educated, you work in a university and your future is going to be a lot different from these guys here.'

Obviously, I had confronted these objections many times before: after every public talk I have ever given, I have been made to answer for my temerity – a white man studying blacks, the very idea!

Rastas, of course, were similarly cautious about my pretensions to understanding from the inside, but they were prepared to suspend judgement until the finished product was available. I had always told them, somewhat haughtily: 'We need something positive written on the movement which people will take notice of. If we wait for a Rasta to do it, we'll be waiting forever.'

In my zeal, I had missed what was possibly one of the most important reactions to this manner of reasoning. When I had justified my research, one Rasta merely retorted: 'Me no want you to understand Rasta; it is I's faith, it is my life.'

And, on another broadly similar occasion, a rather angry Rasta cut deeply: 'What you need to know about Rasta? Him no want to know about you, so why you interested in him.'

I confess the relevance of these statements was lost on me at the time. So searching was my commitment and so pressing were my practical problems that I had little time to consider the ramifications. They were not at the forefront of our minds when Troyna and I conceived our *Black Youth* project. But, as we now put together the final package, uncertainties make us doubt the validity, worth and, indeed, morality of the whole enterprise.

The two unsettling contentions I encountered from the white coach and the black footballer have made me think that the waters in which Troyna and I thought we were steering our craft are unnavigable. We had earned our intellectual compasses and were at the ready to sail amidst turbulent conditions to the shores of understanding. It was a chancy voyage, anyway, and even the hardiest and most willing of seamen can lose direction or sail round in circles.

Whether our project is a circular one, I still do not know; but I am wiser in many respects. I realise that the social gulf which lies between white academic researchers and young blacks is precarious. The reader may feel, even at this point, that the book *Black Youth* is already plummeting to the bottom of an abyss.

Young blacks did not write this work, so one is faced with the fact that it was written in a variety of different perspectives, none of which may do much justice to the views of the youngsters themselves. The book is a collection of guesswork. Systematic, informed and well-articulated guesswork, but guesswork nevertheless. And for this reason alone I would suggest that the reader retain a certain dubiety when digesting the chapters.

Also, young blacks may not read this book and, as both Troyna and I are aware of this – and were always aware of it – we are guilty of trying to produce a work to be read by people who want to understand black youth. As I was forcibly reminded, 'blacks know about what it's like to be black'. So is it important to write a book about people simply to facilitate understanding, appreciation, perhaps to promote sympathy and even to pave the way to helping them? We are, of course, imposing our will on young blacks. We believe – and, as professional researchers, have an interest in believing – that knowledge in itself is a valuable commodity, as nuclear physics and microtechnology are valuable. The purposes knowledge is made to serve may not be so valuable and, on occasion, may be destructive.

This point was underlined in what I thought was an exaggerated way by a black sportsman, who speculated on the results of my research and how they might be employed: 'All you're doing is giving whites the means to keep the blacks down. It's understanding, all right; but it can be used to control.'

Knowledge is a form of control, of course, and, really, social scientists who challenge their world by seeking out new ways of understanding it are increasing the sophistication of control, albeit inadvertently. It is an inescapable trap that even the most critical, emancipatory knowledge can be put to purposes quite at variance to the original schemes of its conceivers.

The knowledge that we proffer in this volume carries no guarantee that it may not be used for manipulative purposes. We accept that responsibility and qualify it simply by stating at the outset that we harbour involvements with the betterment of black youth. We believe that there are problems unique to young blacks and this work is about exposing these problems. In this way, we contend, improvements can be made. They *can*; we do not have the knowledge to suggest whether they will or not.

So: we proceed, imposing our fundamentally different values on others, engaging ourselves in the expansion of a consciousness others might prefer to see contracted. Presumably, black youth want their life-chances improved; so we do share something in common. For all its faults, *Black Youth* is, at least, a start.

'What will you do next?' a black youth recently asked me. 'I suppose you'll finish this project and then look around and think, "oh yes, there's the Asians, they've got a few problems. I think I'll go and study them."' His remark was intended to undermine, even devastate, my whole commitment to the area of race relations, a term I find increasingly restrictive. He was indicating – not unreasonably – that my work was futile.

I took his point and could offer him no convincing evidence to the contrary. Only that I am more comfortable in a world in which futile attempts at improving race relations are made than in a world in which there are no attempts at all.

2 Black Youth in Crisis

ERNEST CASHMORE and
BARRY TROYNA

So Long as You're Black

As the 1970s drew to a close, apprehension mounted in regard to black youth in England. Maybe they were expected to exhibit docility, indifference to what was going on about them, resign themselves to social circumstances. If there was optimism about their ability or inclination to integrate fully into the society which had played host to their parents, it faded as the years passed by. The society did not seem to accommodate their often bizarre needs and if there was a script complete with roles for young blacks, the youngsters themselves clearly did not read it, less still comply with it.

Instead of dutifully bowing to the liberal requirements of a multi-ethnic society, black youths reacted in a volatile fashion: collectively, they promoted a social problem the likes of which had not been provided by any group in the history of migration to England. The futility of technical measures directed at avoiding the type of furores caused by blacks in the USA in the 1960s became apparent as unemployment grew disproportionately amongst this group, street offence and theft convictions spiralled ominously, feelings of disengagement intensified (see Chapters 5 and 6). From the ghettos, emerged a special group, a group which did not regard itself as having a problem, not one which could be resolved through conventional measures, anyway.

Black youth became objects of consternation: accounts of fecklessness, improvidence, violence, laziness and dishonesty were not uncommon and there were indications that West Indians did not bring up their children in a completely satisfactory manner with dire consequences for subsequent achievements at school.

Perspectives on the problematic nature of young blacks were provided by simple comparison with another major ethnic group – Asians. Studies suggested that the first wave of Asians to England were materially in much the same position as West Indians; further, they housed similar expectations as to what they might get out of the new society: a relatively smooth reception, better living conditions, possibly an accumulation of wealth followed by a return to the homeland (see Daniel, 1968; Lawrence, 1974). Objectively, the position of Asians was in alignment with that of West Indians: both groups crystallised in the less salubrious regions of urban centres where housing was most available but least desirable.

Discernibly, the Asians made most inroads in the commercial sphere, establishing small businesses, retail outlets, wholesale and manufacturing services, and many grew to prosperity. West Indians, on the other hand, seemed anchored. Young Asians, highly motivated by their parents to work steadfastly at school and maximise the benefits they might receive from formal education, improved quite dramatically. The emphasis on education in Asian culture had its effect on them and, by the late 1970s, they were comfortably in range of white schoolchildren in terms of actual achievements. Educationally, they were unquestionably well equipped and, in our view, poised to outstrip young whites in attainments (see, for example, Taylor, 1973).

The picture was very different for black youth, very, very different. Study after study (with one conspicuous exception – Driver, 1980) led to the depressing conclusion that young blacks were making little or no impression. Continually, they achieved less than both whites and Asians and there were utterly no grounds for expecting a change. If anything, black youths seemed to be reinforcing their own lack of achievements by consciously promoting an attitude of rejection of education. Whether the lack of achievement bred the loss of affiliation or vice versa is a chicken-and-egg conundrum; for the moment, however, we rest with the observations that young blacks did not do well at school and their orientations to education were such that they gave no cause for believing they would do better in the future. In brief, they did not want to know.

Depicted is a scene where Asian youths, supported by their parents, entertained positive orientations towards education and improved steadily in terms of actual achievements. The importance of formal education as a route to social mobility and material gain was not lost on Asians as it seemingly was on blacks. Their collective attitudes towards education was captured nicely by a black youth whom one of us encountered whilst engaged in research in the late 1970s: 'Education. What good is that to the black man? Qualifications? Them mean nothing *so long as you're black.*'

'So long as you're black': the germinal insight into the dis-affiliation, perhaps? Certainly, we would contend that the social separation of young blacks in the period in question was fomented by the awareness of being black, of being a different colour to the majority of the population and, critically, realising that the blackness could be used as a basis for exclusion. Once this awareness had been broached, the quality of blackness was fused with new significance; it was no longer a superficial, unimportant, what biologists would call 'phenotypical', characteristic. On the contrary, it took on social significance, became a symbol. Being black meant many different things to different people, but there was common apprehension: it meant being different.

One of the features of black youth which interests us is the question of black-gang formation: why did young blacks hang around together rather than with whites or Asians? To offer the conclusion that whites and, for that matter, Asians shut them out, leaving black youths to congregate on their own is facile; we credit young blacks with an active contribution. They did not particularly want to mix and so involuted.

Why? Well, the question is complex and possible answers are implicit in the rest of this chapter but, in general terms, the conclusion reached in one of our studies in Midland and London schools seems serviceable, 'this withdrawal into racially exclusive peer groups results from the pupils' realisation of a common identity and shared destiny' (Troyna, 1978a, p. 64).

Arrogant, rumbustious, contemptuous towards whites – these were some of the popular traits attributed to young blacks. They were not far off the mark. Young blacks retreated into their gangs where they cultivated postures *vis-à-vis* the rest of society and those postures could have been bespoken to engender these kind of negative responses. Too long have sentimental journalists and liberal social investigators emphasised the black man as the receiver of pressures or the reactor to conditions. Well-meaning they may be, but we try not to let naïveté cloud our conception of the black youth. What we wish to do is stress the constructive element of these postures. Black youths were not simply jettisoned out of the mainstream of society and left to survive at the margins; they were not smashed around by the big bad bats of society like ping-pong balls. Generally, they developed and refined their owwn attitudes, orientations and postures in relation to the rest of society.

In this sense, they created their own problems. True, they faced the pressures: racialism was rife (Marsh, 1976); we do not suggest otherwise. But balanced appreciation is required. Young blacks actively and deliberately contributed to their own positions. They were a cultural phenomenon and cultures do not evolve spontaneously: they are worked at, constructed. Let us not fail to take into account the parts played by the blacks in provoking the outcast label slapped on them. They *were* arrogant, rumbustious and contemptuous. And perhaps with good reason.

We do not intend to bleed the black youth of his life; we intend to give him full credit and, as such, we want to accentuate the active part he played. 'Subject to racism, discrimination and endless pressure' (as the cover blurb of Ken Pryce's book, 1979, has it) the black youths might have been, yet their chaotic, powerful culture was a response filled with vim. Linking social conditions to such responses is one of our tasks and, in the process of doing this, we hope to provide insights into the possible consequences of young blacks' stances towards society and the future they might lead to, a future which may well be presaged by the occurrences at Bristol in 1980 and Brixton in 1981.

Briefly, we choose to see insecurely rooted black youths, prematurely matured and sprouting in a cultural marshland of wall-daubed tower blocks and inner-city areas, educated on words which they find irrelevant – and do not know how to spell anyway. Occasionally, they are stimulated by images and strike up postures, often of sudden violence. With their relations with the police in a state of decay, they make accusations of harassment and brutality – in their own words, 'oppression' – but get pilloried by the media, ignored by politicians and slammed by the ranters of the racist right or recruited as mercenaries of the revolutionary left.

That many authors have withdrawn from the type of conclusion we shall reach in the coming pages is forgivable. Such is the climate in which we write that more socially satisfying convictions are better received. We all know that there is a problem surrounding young blacks – do they know it? Some schools of thought hold that they do and they argue further that they know of a solution. Maybe they do; let us see.

The Other Half of the Story

There was a joke doing the rounds at the start of the 1980s; it was usually received by a volley of guffaws followed by a sprinkling of earnest and acknowledging applause. It went: 'I see they're showing *Roots* on TV again; this time, they're running it backwards so that it'll have a happy ending!'

This joke reveals quite a lot about English culture and collective attitudes towards blacks (more than some volumes of social scientific theorising), but it is a strange irony that its implicit theme would have found relevance in the black community. Insulting to many it might have been, treacherous in its implication and jocular fuel for followers, blatant or latent, of the National Front or British Movement; but interesting also to a great many commentators on young blacks who formulated what they considered viable and, indeed, inevitable schemes to alleviate problems connected with black youth.

Briefly stated, the television adaptation of Alex Haley's semi-autobiographical work serialised the development of an African family, devastated by capture, forced migration, enslavement and, later, racialism, from eighteenth-century West Africa to contemporary USA. Roots were what the author was able to unearth when pulling up his family tree: the underground fibres he found in African culture, a culture flourishing and fertile before the onslaught of the slave traders. Running the film backwards would leave the blacks of the USA and, for that matter, the UK back in Africa.

The sentiment has been given articulate expression by blacks themselves, most pertinently by the Jamaican Marcus Garvey whose 'Back to Africa' scheme found support from (he reckoned) 4 million North American and West Indian blacks in the 1920s. His ideas were transformed into an apocalyptic vision by sections of his followers, members of the Rastafarian movement who saw the 'return' to Africa – to them synonomous with Ethiopia – as the redemptive consummation of history, a time when the social cosmos was to be turned over and all blacks restored to their rightful 'Fatherland'.

The movement, which began in Jamaica in the early 1830s, gained currency in the urban centres of England in the late 1970s and was, certainly in our view, the most important cultural development in the West Indian presence. Its members, the Rastas, totally dissociated themselves from society and entertained the ideas of a new Africa based on an Arcadian vision; such a vision informed the stances they assumed: often hostile to the wider society characterised as Babylon, and definitely not interested in engaging in the type of negotiation which might lead to integration – such a concept was out of tune with Rastafarian ideals.

Obviously, the movement represented an extreme culture of disenchantment and resistance to mainstream society and we do not intend to exaggerate its pervasiveness. On the other hand, nothing can diminish its general importance to black youth. The movement's ideas were vitriolic: they burned through existing patterns of West Indian beliefs and provided new ways of viewing the world and the place of black people in that world. Many of those ideas were taken up, often critically, by other young blacks. Rastas were ridiculed, dismissed, even rejected, by other blacks in the UK; but they were never ignored. Even those critical of the type of views held by Rastas were forced to bring their attentions to focus on that group of youths. So controversial were they that they demanded attention in one way or another (See Cashmore, 1979a).

'Africa', 'Zion', 'Babylon', 'I and I' were terms incorporated in the young blacks' vocabularies. They may not have held so much relevance for them as they held for the Rastas, but they were illuminating nevertheless and the concept of the black man having a rich cultural heritage buried deep beneath the over-lapping layers of colonialism spread throughout the young black community. The conception informed a new consciousness and one which many commentators thought would have to be addressed lest the energy firing it be wasted or changed into something more sinister.

The strain of reasoning ran thus: black kids were growing in their collective awareness of being black and therefore, at source, Arican. Television shows like *Roots* were seen to reinforce that awareness. First-generation West Indians may have been too preoccupied with the practical problems of existence to indulge in such biographical wanderings, but their sons and daughters developed a different way of looking at themselves. They did not have to be Rastas to understand that they were truly displaced Africans; possibly they grew mindful of Peter Tosh's reminder: 'Don't care where you come from, as long as you're a black man, you're an African' (from the song 'African' on the *Equal Rights* album, CBS, published by ATV Music, 1977). All the discontents and difficulties associated with young blacks could be reduced to the fact that, according to this argument, they had realised their 'Africanness'. But black youth had no channels along which they could explore the possibilities of that realisation.

They thought that they were denied the opportunities to learn more about African cultures, that continent's religions, its leaders and their achievements, the way in which European colonialism had destroyed the civilisation leaving hollowness or imposing new realities of slavery. Extending this argument, it was posited that there existed an urgent desire on behalf of black youths to gain more knowledge of Africa and, therefore, of themselves or, at least, their predecessors – the *Roots* story writ large.

A Rasta once tapped the mood perfectly: quoting Bob Marley he reckoned, 'It's not all that glitters is gold, *half the story has never been told*'. It was, according to many concerned with young blacks, the other half of the story which needed telling.

Policy implications were fairly unambiguous: give black youth the opportunities to learn about Africa and instil in them a sense of dignity, even pride, in being African. That would have the effect of balancing out the alleged 'white bias' in English education.

A way of assuaging the problem was to set up provision for black or Afro-study groups, or augment conventional education with such curricular, or even extra-curricular items, possibly establishing independent cultural study centres and encouraging all-black projects. Young blacks were to have made available to them the means to study Africa, its history, culture, and so on – the other half of the story. Through immersion into these kinds of ventures, it was thought that the youths would grow aware of their heritage and themselves; they would find the raw material for identities and generate a sense of pride in being black. The thrust was essentially to involve young blacks, make them aware and direct their efforts into something positive and profitable to themselves rather than squander them in the less reputable seams of the black community.

Operationally, the plans were to integrate black studies into all school curricula so that white schoolchildren and all other ethnic groups would be made to engage in the studies. In this way, it was thought that a broad range of enlightenment would be accomplished; black youth were to glean what Robert Jeffcoate called *Positive Image* (1979). All round, the schoolchildren would get to know each other better and this understanding would lead to more harmonious relations between them.

Also, more objectivity would follow. Instead of the European being represented as the benevolent, zealous carrier of the 'white man's burden', patronisingly uplifting the morals of African heathens, he was to appear as the fearsome, profiteering slave-trader, slicing apart cultures without any compunction in his effort to produce capital. A more realistic scenario would thus be achieved. Also, the underplayed features of African development and politics in post-colonial years would be stressed.

Similar contents might have been used in the autonomous self-help groups devoted to the promotion of such educational ideals. The aim here was to give the youths the idea that they were not only recipients of learning but also participants to it. All-black projects with no outside interferences were the goal.

For some, a panacea, for others a strategy of containment, the black studies programmes were championed virtually without objection. Few commentators voiced a protest against them and, indeed we, too, were sold on the idea in the late 1970s – that is, before we realised their limitations.

Of the more persuasive advocates, Raymond Giles stands out. His investigation into teachers' perceptions of the special educational needs of black primary and secondary-school children in socially disadvantaged areas of the Inner London Education Authority led him to three broad recommendations based on the black community's response to 'racism in the form of prejudice and discrimination' (1977, p. 154). They were:

(1) A need for black unity and development of a positive concept among Britain's West Indian population of African descent.
(2) A need for new programmes and courses of study in schools with sizeable percentages of students from West Indian backgrounds who consider themselves to be black.
(3) A need to distinguish between social class prejudice and racism as factors related to the educational disadvantage of black people in Britain.

Two approaches occurred to Giles (1977, pp. 163–4). Either a curriculum revision: 'The inclusion of themes and topics which relate to multi-cultural Britain rather than a concentration on cultures and lifestyles in communities abroad.' Or, more radically, 'to increase home school compatability (*sic*) and help *students of the West Indian background*' (our emphasis). 'Obviously, there is a need for children born in Britain but continually referred to as being different and not accepted because of colour to develop a positive self-image and identity as well as a sense of pride in being black in a society where this is not valued.' Giles believed that this might best be handled through 'supplementary school programmes or extra-curricular activities' and that 'specialists' could be brought into the schools for the purpose of implementing the black studies. Interestingly, and unlike Jeffcoate, he felt no particular 'need' for education of this nature to be made compulsory for whites or any other colour students.

Embittered possibly by the failure of any educational authority to take up the type of ideas proposed by Giles and others with any commitment, some groups took it on themselves to meet the central requirements of such black study programmes. The imperative was retained. 'It has been clear that in order for black children to realise their real potential they must be respected as equal participants capable of full educational attainment', stated the first Annual Report of the Afro-Caribbean Educational Resource Project (ACER), which began work in 1976. It went on, 'the identity of a child or what he inherits is important to his or her self-esteem; to deny this is to deprive the individual of a basic human right. The school should become an enriched inter-cultural learning environment for the non-racist society that we all hope for' (1977, p. 4). Noble sentiments and ones which gain the approval of Giles.

The ACER wanted 'structural change' in education, 'multi-cultural material' made available for schoolchildren and 'a well rounded educative experience for all pupils in their school life'. Its initiative was to seek funding from various sources in order to set up an educational body, complete with resources – however limited – capable of providing an independent alternative to what the young blacks had on offer to them.

Working along parallel lines, some organisations set about establishing supplementary education for black youths. One of the most successful outfits, the Dachwying Parents Association in Peckham, London, ran regular Saturday morning study groups for about fifty or sixty children and youths. (Though we point out that Parents' Associations were by no means unanimous in their support of such schemes: witness the disquiet caused by the Lambeth West Indian Parents Association after *The Natty Dread Colouring Book*, an uncritical publication about Rastas, was introduced into some borough schools.)

The attempts perhaps obviated some of the problems which may have bedevilled a straightforward application of Giles's principles, for, as Joanna Mack pointed out, 'supplementary services – though important as a temporary fill-in while schools are failing West Indian pupils – do not tackle the root of the problem. Namely: changing the thinking of schools' (1977, p. 512).

The implication is that most black studies integrated pro-grammes are based on precarious premises. This is clear enough: to change schoolchildren's ideas is one thing, but changing the teachers' is where the crunch comes. There is more interest in compensating the pupils rather than changing the school. But then both approaches suffer from this weakness. Neither offers much more than a rather cosmetic improvement: they might cover up a few blemishes and effect a number of beautifications; but they leave the real infection lying beneath the surface awaiting eruption.

With the intentions of these programmes we have no quarrel; the question of desirability and implication we find debatable. We feel that to impose such broad cartoon outlines on serious social issues dissipates rather than concentrates the cultural impact which young blacks have to make. To clog them with stodgy apathetic images of a forelorn Africa, virginal and untainted by the noxious influences of the rapacious Europeans is to place them on a landscape which owes more to fantasy than actuality.

Black or Afro-studies portray the black man as a courageous, skilful, intelligent creator of his own culture, a worshipper of his own gods, a politician of acuity and unremitting independence. His continent was one of prosperity and one which, if left alone by whites, would surely have flourished. This is not falsification but it is more a satisfying picture, an exaggerated representation highlighting certain, selected characteristics while neglecting others, than a graphic reminder that this *was* reality, it is no longer reality and has no necessary connection with life in England in the late twentieth century – not even for blacks.

Imbuing black youth with a sense of heritage, a feeling that they have cultural antecedents, and were not spontaneously ejected from a cultural vacuum is all very well. Let them know they stopped off at some impressive watering holes before arriving on the contemporary scene. Blacks in the USA have shown the value of elevating one's Africanness and experiencing it as something positive and beneficial. But there are limitations and there are dangers.

Limited in the sense that, as we pointed out, the studies leave the broader problems untouched and attend merely to cosmetic issues, compensating the young blacks by diverting their attentions to a history rather than a present. Dangerous they must be seen to be because, in creating a sense of identity and hence solidarity, they can have a polarising effect.

We acknowledge the deficiencies in the school system, but think that to deflect black youths' intellectual energies in alternative directions may well alienate them further from a world for which they have little love anyway. Building black study programmes into existing curricula does not necessarily lead to an increased affinity for the more conventional elements of education, a grasp of which we tend to believe is a prerequisite for some measure of meaningful progress to be made in society.

Black and Afro-studies may well exacerbate an already polarising situation in which blacks eagerly lap up the Afro-education even to the point of emphasising their differentness. But, while we are not so-called assimilationists by any criteria, we see hidden dangers. Differentness in itself is not harmful. But, allied to certain postures and attitudes, it can be divisive. Whilst not being totally dismissive of black studies propagators and their aims, we cannot be enthusiastic about the futures of the projects themselves. The real issues remain untouched by their efforts and those very efforts may well prove destructive to relationships between young blacks and the rest of society in the longer term. The black studies are, in our opinion, cosmetic in function and their masters myopic.

Because They Are Young

The fact that young blacks generally developed attitudes, values, stances, styles of life that can be described as running counter to dominant culture has not intrigued some commentators overly. One of the reasons for this being so is that they see the type of difficulties posed by black youths as generational, as residing in the 'youth' as against the 'black'. They seem problematic because they are young and *all* children go through stages of maturation when they grow tense with their parents and dissatisfied with the wider society, even uncomfortable with their own sense of identity.

Black youths were seen to go through exactly the same generational turbulence as the Teds in the 1950s, the mods and rockers in the 1960s, the punks in the 1970s and the constellation of mod revivalists, come-back skinheads, rude boys, new romantics – you name it – in the early 1980s. The pattern in which youth 'cultures' (or 'subcultures' as Hebdige, 1979, prefers to call them) surface, then sink, then resurface, then sink again suggests a regurgitating cycle of squabbles between generations; but more often than not, the culture which seemed so vital and formidable in the June of one year seems either commercial, comical or just irrelevant by the December of the next.

They look to be irritating but ephemeral indulgences: give youth free rein and the cultures will disappear with maturational reform.

Such cultures could be said to possess an inbuilt obsolescence and so, on reflection, were not worth too much attention, a viewpoint obviously not shared by the media which, over the years, have contributed vigorously in creating the youthful 'folk devils' and the communal 'moral panics' which usually accompany them (see Cohen, 1973). Young blacks were folk devils in their own rights (see Troyna, 1977b). Rastas were the most vivid and spectacular attestations to the supposed diablerie, but other black youths also seemed mischieviously affected by the devil's handiwork (for an example of this view, see J. Brown, 1977). 'Difficulties' would be an accurate assessment of the state of young blacks' lives; problems would suggest something more serious – they would presumably outgrow their statuses. If these perceived difficulties are to be regarded as no different from those of white youth, or youngsters of any colour and from any background, and the issue is generational not ethnic nor racial, then the conclusion must be reached that they are not worth bothering about. Reform will come with age.

Our argument starts from the contention that there is something special about the experience of being black and that this experience structures the position of black youth. We have drawn on our own empirical work to suggest that, as young blacks become aware of their colour and realise that it can be depreciated and used as a basis for exclusion, they fuse this blackness with a new significance, incorporate it into their consciousness, organise their subjective biographies so as to include it, strike up allegiances and perceive adversaries on the understanding of it; in general, position themselves in relation to that quality of blackness. Further, we contend that the apprehension of being black and of being different because of it becomes clearer as the youth proceeds through his post-school years; the encounter with the wider society reinforces rather than weakens the salience. Social experience gives support to the belief that blackness means being different, usually in an inferior way. That apprehension does not wash away with the years as if written in sand with a stick before the tide breaks; it has a lasting efficacy.

Youth counselling and associated services could be employed as remedial measures aimed at lubricating the youth's passages through the rocky years, but how can one set about conquering the experiences of unemployment, or what Pryce inelegantly calls 'shit work', friction-packed relations with the police, living in run-down areas of the inner cities? These are the social pressure spots where the dimension of blackness becomes transposed onto the generational problems of youth.

And it is this dimension which separates young blacks from their white counterparts. Youth has its own problems; being black its own problems; put them together and you have a whole new set of problems which tend to dispel the optimism of those who believe rather sanguinely that youthful exuberance will subside as maturity comes to the fore. We understand these problems to have a more solid potential.

Seeing the Bars and Chains

Many of the confusions elicited from the previous arguments stem from a simplified conception of black youths, the cultures they have devised and developed and the meaning they attach to them. Young blacks in the late 1970s and early 1980s had a plethora of cultural alternatives available to them and their commitment to any one or more of them might have been total or segmental. They housed a variety of different orientations to different cultures. Furthermore, a culture could mean different things to different people; what the youth got out of his involvement with the culture depended on his subjective biography and his experience with the world.

We have argued for an appreciation of the patterned nature of young blacks' experience of the social world, an experience forged in the encounter with blackness, the realisation of this quality and the meaning which it acquired in later school and post-school years. Shape and definition were given to blackness; and conceptions of the self and of other black youths were ordered accordingly. Social arrangements revolved around being black; the sense of shared destiny, as we called it, was heightened in importance. And it was out of this accumulation of experiences of the link between blackness, differentness and, crucially, disprivilege, that the culture of disengagement emerged.

But, critically, that made up only part of the wider cultural complex in which the youths might have been interested. The street-corner gang member may have lived at home quite satisfactorily in comfortable domestic circumstances; he may have attended black discothèques yet have had a white girlfriend; he may have hung around with others who disregarded the educational systems and still carried on at school or college; he may have criticised the oppressive white dominance of Babylon but still have worked as an electrical engineer in a white-owned company from 9 till 5. He may, as one youth we knew, have held very vehement views on the exploitative structures of white control and its inevitable demise and the hopelessness of the black cause until that day, yet continue to work sedulously taking advantage of government training schemes to improve his professional qualifications.

Basically, our point is simple: young blacks always had and still have, their fingers in a number of cultural pies and to assign them to specific categories known as lifestyles such as 'Hustlers', 'Proletarian Respectables', or 'Mainliners' (as Pryce does) is tantamount to freezing a frame and studying it while the movie is still running – you miss the interesting bits. Our investigations indicate that black youth did not and does not adopt one cultural lifestyle, but mix many. So it would be feasible to expect the ostensibly docile bakery worker to be a hostile critic of white society, a part-time pimp, a Pentecostalist church member and the organiser of an all-black, self-help group. He does not have to belong to one culture; he may belong to many.

The importance of this is that we can acknowledge that a great many black youths do not immerse themselves in cultures of apparent disengagement, the vivid, extreme example of which would be the Rastafarian movement, but seemingly integrate into mainstream occupations, work towards qualifications, entertain harmonious relations with whites; but, beyond this, we contend that the crucial realisation of being different, being black, remains. Marks are made, and impressions of the consciousness affect the way in which the black youth perceives his world.

For all his efforts, indeed his achievements, he knows he is black: that colour is part of his identity and he knows that this will ultimately affect his life-chances. And this gives him a sort of unity even if he does not wish to acknowledge it. We believe that black youths' lifestyles, or cultures, are diverse and contain a wide variety of aspirations, orientations and commitments and that the youths themselves may be involved in many, but between them is a cultural tie. It unites the office worker to the Rastaman and, given the right circumstances, it becomes evident. It already has done so in Bristol and elsewhere.

One way in which it might become evident is through organisation along political lines and many commentators have shown sensitivity to this possibility (see Phizacklea and Miles, 1980). It involves a change of perception, seeing problems of day-to-day existence as derived not so much from the white man as from the system of which he is part. Such a change is nicely captured in Horace Ove's movie, *Pressure*, which traces the attempts of Tony, the English-born son of Trinidadians, to find employment after successfully completing GCE examinations. His brother, who was born in Trinidad, is a member of a black power organisation and criticises Tony for his accommodating attitude towards whites. After successive experiences estrange him from his white friends, Tony casually attends a meeting of his brother's associates where he remarks that not all whites are bad. His brother responds: 'Who controls politics, big business, etc.?' But Tony follows the logic revealing to himself, as well as the others, that only a very few whites are holders of positions of power and the majority are in basically the same position as blacks: 'They're colonised, too; just like us. The only difference is that *we see the bars and chains.*'

It was a sort of transition in consciousness, a passing to the apprehension of problems endemic to black life as caused by the structure of relationships which held some groups in positions of power, prestige and authority, and others out of them. Pressure describes the result of processes transcending the capabilities of any one human being. Therefore, to relieve it, there needs to be an attack at higher levels; and to mount such an attack needs organisation – political organisation. If the solution to the undesirable situation is political, it needs to be tackled politically.

Excited by the prospect of a collective realisation of this, commentators, many from the left, have savoured the possibility

and encouraged the probability of young blacks growing desperate and frustrated at their own inability to instigate changes in
their own conditions and looking to avenues along which to
explore alternatives. The political avenue beckons.

Militant political and quasi-political movements are by no
means new to the black community in the UK. Their history can
be traced back to the early 1960s when such figures as Michael de
Freitas (also known as Michael Abdul Malik and Michael X) and
Obi Egbuna stirred up nests of hornets with their inflammatory
organisations modelled on the American black power groups.
British equivalents of the Black Panthers and the Nation of
Islam, better known as the Black Muslims, came to prominence
and their leaders were strident in their calls for changes, despite
their numerically unimpressive memberships. Both de Freitas
and Egbuna had celebrated clashes with the law, de Freitas
eventually being hanged in Trinidad.

Not that either organisation really caught on in such a way as
to provoke large-scale movements comparable with those in the
USA. By the end of the 1960s, every black political group of any
note had been subdued and the leaders rendered ineffective.
Nevertheless, 'the seeds of consciousness had been scattered', as
one Birmingham-based West Indian put it.

Since that time there have been a number of black political or
'fringe' political organisations, some liberal, others revolutionary, and still others very revolutionary. Hostility to whites
seemed dependent on the amount of Marxist input to the ideology. For example, some groups saw themselves as part of the
wider working-class struggle against bourgeois capitalism, while
others thought the black struggle to be an independent one and,
therefore, resisted engaging in any kind of venture with whites; a
member of the Afro-Caribbean organisation in Handsworth
expressed his movement's view: 'History shows that the whites
have never done the blacks any favours. They organise their
whole system so that, even when they're doing them good, they're
really keeping them down. What reasons can you give me for
thinking this will ever change?'

Muhammad Ali once gave his explanation for this kind of
thinking (presuming it needs explanation), suggesting that a nest
of vipers may have only one venomous snake; but who can ask a
man putting his hand into the nest to differentiate. Put differently, tell a black that not every white is bad, but do not expect
him to be bothered to sort out the good from the not-so-good at his
own expense.

There have been one or two revealing instances of black
political mobilisation and there is no question about the potential

collective consciousness, apprehension of problems and situations common to black people, which could be dovetailed into straight-forward political manœuvres. The Race Today Collective and the Bradford Blacks Collective are examples, but the most vivid came in 1981 with the mass protest against the police's handling of the inquiry into the deaths of thirteen black youths at Deptford, London. Despite these, we do not believe that any formal political mobilisation of young blacks is probable; and our reasons derive from our understanding of a different form of consciousness which swept through the black community. The source of the new awareness was the Rastafarian movement, members of which coined the term Babylon to characterise the society in which they existed, some would say 'suffered'. In Rastas' eyes, the world which surrounded them was fraught with evil; only they had the perceptual equipment to see this. Since the early days of slavery, the colonising Europeans had sought to dominate blacks. Initially, through purely physical means – forced slavery – they succeeded, but after emancipation, subtler methods were called for and so they offered black European religions which were ill-suited to the interests of blacks, political systems which effectively excluded blacks from articulating protest, and economic structures at the bottom of which blacks were riveted. The Babylonian system had a self-perpetuating basis in which the whites continued to control and the blacks accepted their legitimate right to do so. In other words, blacks contributed to their own subordination.

Throughout the late 1970s, young blacks saw the rise of such ideas among their peers and, for each new believer in Babylon, the plausibility of it increased. Even for those too young to take full comprehension of the events around them, the ideas connected with Babylon took an ill-defined shape. Picture a gang of five black schoolchildren and two older black youths walking together as a Panda car draws alongside; two police officers jump out and whisk off the older youths; the car draws away to screams of 'Babylon, Babylon!' from the schoolchildren. This scene, witnessed in Birmingham, captures what we understand to be the pervasive nature of the idea of Babylon. Even to those untutored in political theory, the idea of Babylon as a palpable reality constraining and suppressing blacks gained purchase (for a discussion of this, see Cashmore, 1981).

Now, if you believe in Babylon, one implication is that you believe it cannot be conquered through conventional political measures. It exists as a massive, immutable structure and has a capacity to repel or absorb attacks. Such is its nature which has been refined for the best part of four hundred years. You also believe that to organise politically and attempt to change the position of blacks through prescribed means is futile and self-defeating. What might appear at one level to be a change for the better, an improvement in the lot of black people is, at another, simply a piecemeal adjustment, leaving the fundamentals of white control intact. The system is equipped to neutralise challenges levelled at it on its own terms.

And, after all, black political organisations, for all their protestations, ultimately have to negotiate; and negotiation means exchanging with Babylon.

The idea of Babylon was a growing one in the black community in the late 1970s and early 1980s and it was a serviceable model for rendering intelligible everyday experiences. Bad deals at school, few employment opportunities, sour relations with the police: these were perfectly explicable by reference to Babylon. But the idea tended to undermine the credibility of political groups; maybe it seemed better to contain the bitterness, the rage, and wait, rather than risk emasculation at the master's hands.

Perhaps we overestimate the importance of Babylon, or even misinterpret the nature of the ideas and how they might in future change to yield a straightforward political discharge. But we understand the action implications of believing in the existence of Babylon to militate against the political organisation and, whilst not wishing to sound critical less still censorious, of the black groups dedicated to political ideas, we feel that they will not attract the mass of black youth, but only a minority committed to political ideals, those who see the bars and chains and think that they have the tools with which to smash them.

The Turning-Point

It is almost axiomatic that young blacks do badly at school, grow disenchanted, then slip into twilight zones where such activities as thieving or hustling are acceptable or even *de rigueur*. As a black youth expressed it to Melanie Phillips: 'Thievin' means survival ... When your schooling's gone wrong, there's no jobs because the firm down the road's chucked out all its blacks and you're on the streets, then thieving's the only way you can survive' (1976, p. 166). And, in a similar vein, Stuart Hall and his colleagues have argued that 'the educational system has served effectively to depress the general opportunities for employment and educational advancement and has therefore resulted in reproducing the young black worker as labour at the lower end of employment, production and skill' (1978, p. 346).

The same authors reckon that the black 'labouring class' spends time 'doing nothing, filling out time, trying to survive', so an obvious strategy for survival is petty crime 'eventually culminating in becoming a substitute job' (1978, p. 359). In this sense, 'crime is politically viable'.

The question we ask is: For how long will it continue to be viable? We accept that the hustling–street crime type of existence is commonplace amongst black youth and this type of activity is attracting recruits as regularly as young blacks drop out at school – and that is regularly (see Bagley, 1979). But there is a point at which these operations or strategies for survival will become inadequate methods for maintaining a foothold, however precarious, in society: they lose viability. Then what will happen?

As a way of answering this, let us go over the various elements at work in black youth culture. First, objective conditions. Failures at school, a sense of dissatisfaction with education generally breeding badly educated, unqualified youths without outstanding prospects in the occupational world and with good chances of protracted unemployment – chances often enhanced by a reluctance to take employment. So, let us stress the active part played in the unemployment: the dissatisfaction with school broadens into a dissatisfaction with society generally which, in turn, translates into a desire to have nothing to do with it. This is given momentum by the apprehension of being black and therefore sharing the problems common to all black people in the UK. This means coming to terms with being black and being different and the spread of the idea of Babylon and all its implications tends to make crystal clear the reasons why it is black people who have to share problems. There is a fissure which developed between first-generation West Indians and their sons and daughters and there is no doubt at all that the 'strategies of survival' of street crime, hustling, small-time pimping, and so on are easy options to the black youths; thus the fissure is sent into further disrepair.

There is a complex of cultures created by young blacks and we do not intend to caricature it by suggesting that every black youth opts for the 'strategies of survival' – though, of course, the more visible do. What we have argued is that there is an irreducible, common element of being black which ties black youths together and gives their perceptions of others and themselves sharpness and definition. When all is said and done, they are black and share the experiences of all other blacks in some way.

We understand young blacks to have a sense of impotence: they find the world about them nullifying in that they cannot change their situations, they have neither expertise nor resources. They share a sense of shared destiny, but destiny is controlled by a power that foreordains with inexorable necessity. The belief that the power cannot be beaten, that it is invincible, is given more credibility by the ideas of Babylon. Destiny is in the hands of Babylon and a mood of fatalism is rife in the black community: the young blacks feel that they cannot change things.

The point at which things must be done in order to dissolve this mood of fatalism has arrived. We believe that the attempt to revitalise or restore the ability to instigate change in people's own circumstances is in process. Street crimes and other 'strategies for survival' have only limited use. They are exactly that: ways of surviving, not living; they have no lasting impact and bring no improvement. Political organisation is possible but improbable. When all else fails, violence surfaces.

There is a penchant for violence within the West Indian culture, possibly stemming from the days of slavery when the only method of retaliation was doing physical damage to the overseer, agent or even slave-master. Slave rebellions necessitated a great deal of physical process and, as Lacey has observed on the more contemporary West Indian scene, 'violence is endemic in Jamaican social and political life ... violence is a reaction to acute frustration arising out of economic and social deprivations' (cited in Bagley, 1979, p. 70).

But, whatever the sources of this violent proclivity, there can be no denying its existence: black youths do have a certain fascination for violence. The almost incredible enthusiasm for movies in the *Kung Fu* idiom and the massive numbers involving themselves in the martial arts (as well as the more conventional contact sports) tells us something about young blacks' interest in violence, as does their celebration of a range of archetypal violent anti-heroes, 'Dirty Harry', Chuck Norris and the late Bruce Lee.

The strategies outlined by Hall *et al.* mostly involve some sort of violence, even if it is directed at targets which are unlikely to prove troublesome; and it is conducted collectively so as to remove much chance of repulsion. Street attacks used to be the sovereign operations of black boys but, more recently, girls have organised themselves into gangs and have demonstrated a willingness to engage in such tactics. The growth of the Rebels, as the girls call themselves, suggests some form of rise in female consciousness, of feminism, but interestingly, the route which the girls have taken is in direct emulation of their male counterparts.

Perhaps the violence can be seen as a secondary survival strategy or even a strategy for venting frustrations at not being able to instigate change or neutralise the mood of fatalism, an attempt to 'make something happen'. Perceptions of alternatives may disappear and effectiveness of violence is pointed up. Thus the act is instrumental as a way of discharging frustrations; but perhaps symbolic too: given the currency of Babylon, directed violence could be seen as striking a blow at an oppressive system. There is no doubt that black youth lacks the leverage to conduct a successful campaign for social change. What it has is a capacity to come together and collectively cause disturbances, to disrupt communities for short periods of time.

These are angry young people and there is always the possibility that this mood could be harnessed to organisations; a solid organisation of black youth would be formidable. What is more likely, however, is a series of loosely connected, maybe spontaneous gatherings without overall direction but with enormous potential to disturb.

There have been instances indicating what young blacks can do when their concerns crystallise around specific issues and the possibility of violent scenes is enhanced with every successive round of unqualified school-leavers recruited to the lower orders of the occupational world or registered with the Department of Employment.

Unemployment has been cited as the principal cause of the events at Brixton, as have the police and their policies towards black youth. But, if we are to glean anything from the recent uprisings, it is that young blacks are responding not to specific targets but to the system generally, the system they call Babylon. In all the episodes of the early 1980s, black youths chose to attack the institutions which symbolised their entrapment in the system: houses, shops, cars, the police – but in their immediate environment, not in the more middle-class districts where the targets would have been more obvious and strategic. They attacked in their own neighbourhoods. They tried to destroy the things which surrounded them because they were the very objects which were tangible proofs of the existence of Babylon.

The prospect is not pleasant, but it has to be faced; the situation is dire, but it has to be reckoned with. Measures we have at our disposal are cosmetic: they mask the real discontent beneath the surface. Nothing short of a wholesale transformation of attitudes, orientations and postures towards young blacks and, crucially, on the behalf of young blacks, will suffice in defusing a potentially explosive future. People expect things of black youths and the latter expect things of others; both sets of expectations are usually fulfilled. These expectations are therefore unlikely to be changed and, without such changes, there can only be a further slide into the kind of ugly crisis of violence that we both find abhorrent, yet have unwillingly to concede is a menacing probability.

3 The Manufacture of Marginality

MALCOLM CROSS

It is now commonplace to observe that the children of Britain's non-white population occupy a marginal role in education, employment and other spheres of social and economic life. By 'marginal' in this context is normally meant that they do not fully share in the securities, opportunities and benefits of citizenship. Of course, in this they are not alone. One could take any sphere and find others who, for a variety of reasons, were denied access to those rights which most citizens take as their birthright. However, notwithstanding the claims of women or of the handicapped or the elderly, there is no other subsection of the population that suffers the peculiar congery of difficulties associated with racial or ethnic descent. In this sense exclusion on the periphery is not a specialised handicap, it is a generalised experience constituting a new and inferior form of citizenship.

It is important to separate this phenomenon from immigration. In looking at the issues affecting black youth we are not directly addressing problems associated with immigration. The black youth of Handsworth is, of course, more of a stranger to Jamaica than he is to the West Midlands. While it is true that some Asian youth have language difficulties, these are as much associated with parental demands for literacy in Gujerati and Punjabi as they are for ease in English.

This chapter is not concerned with yet another rehearsal of the evidence on discrimination, as crucial as that evidence is. Rather, it will focus on the apparent resistance of second-class citizenship to succumb to the supposedly universalising tendencies of social policy, with particular reference to the place of black British of West Indian descent. Why does it appear as if the marginality of black youth is 'manufactured' or reproduced? Has social policy magnified or minimised this tendency? The answers to these questions are complex and the chapter will conclude by suggesting some ways in which social policy has confirmed marginality – or possibly even magnified it. This is not to be read as suggesting that all social policies have had this effect, although it does mean that, as presently constituted, policies which might be defended on the grounds of their ability to transcend discrimination must not be uncritically accepted as having done so.

Types of Marginality

To speak of 'second-class' citizenship is to imply that various manifestations of marginality may be compounded but that they are not simply additive. That is, the sum total of marginality has a reality *sui generis* because of the interaction between one form and the next. However, the fact that an absence of jobs for young blacks affects their experience of schooling or their relations with the police, does not prevent us making an analytic distinction between types of marginality. I shall argue that there are four separable zones where marginality can be identified, without suggesting that each has an entirely distinct effect upon the overall problem or that it is not possible to identify many other spheres of equal relevance for social policy. These four forms of marginality are as follows:

> Generational – the marginality of age
> Educational – the marginality of the school experience
> Locational – the marginality of place and space
> Occupational – the marginality of employment

I shall look at each of these in turn and conclude that, on balance, the first two spheres have considerable attention in social policy while the second pair have aroused a far from ready response. I shall argue that the survival of racial marginality, particularly as it affects young people, may be, in part, a function of this apparent inconsistency. That is, marginality may be magnified by intervention in some spheres and manufactured by the lack of it in others.

(1)   *Generational Marginality*

Anthropological and other social research on Caribbean societies is replete with comments on the apparent closeness and durability of kinship ties between the generations. In a classic study of family patterns in Guyana, Raymond Smith observed that 'it is an outstanding fact that the transition from childhood to adult status is almost imperceptible' (Smith, 1956, p. 137). David Lowenthal testifies that 'the tie between parents and children – especially mothers and sons – is closer and more durable than that between most marital partners' (Lowenthal, 1972,

p. 186). Even in London, where migrant history and occupational expectations divide the generations, Nancy Foner recently found that 'by and large, despite the bases for cleavage between young and old Jamaicans, age related differences do not become the basis for sharp and bitter struggles between them' (Foner, 1979, p. 182). Foner goes on to point out that membership of an elaborate, diffuse family system and the common experience of racism unite rather than divide the generations.

This picture is not one, however, that emerges from official agencies. On the contrary, social policy is based on the premise that West Indians suffer from weak family units and that young people are alienated from British society in part by the failure of the family unit to provide support. The implication is normally that there are strong generational differences, perhaps exacerbated by the differing expectations and reference groups adopted by migrants and their offspring. One example among many that could be cited is drawn from the evidence to the Select Committee on Home Affairs, a subcommittee of which is currently considering 'racial disadvantage'. When discussing the problem of young homeless blacks, a member of the committee posed the question to a spokesman of the Department of the Environment whether homelessness could not be considered a 'cultural reaction' rather than a manifestation of poor housing or the necessity to leave home to seek work. A senior official indicated his support for this view on the grounds that family disputes led to young blacks leaving home (HC, 1979–80, 610–vi, para. 679). Without wishing to deny that such cases may exist, it is important to note that no evidence of a greater degree of intergenerational disputes has ever been adduced and nor is it clear that even if it were it could be regarded as a 'cultural' phenomenon.

What is important, however, is the degree to which this thinking has permeated official agencies whose task it is to assist young blacks in overcoming the tensions and difficulties involved in negotiating the isolating and alienating years that in Western societies are defined as 'youth'. For example, a recent research report on youth and race in the inner city sponsored by the National Association of Youth Clubs and funded by the Department of Education and Science (DES) found that official provision of youth facilities was suffused with assumptions that the difficulties faced by young blacks were largely the result of unrealistic aspirations and cultural idiosyncrasies (John, 1980). The empirical work on which this report is based recorded that a large proportion of those in the youth service wrongly perceived their black clients as foreign- rather than British-born. As the report comments:

The outstanding feature of this distorted perception of the group was the way in which officials and professionals employed by statutory agencies believed themselves to be still dealing with West Indians born and bred in a different social and cultural context from that of English society. (John, 1980, p. 66)

Some officials regarded it as inevitable that black youngsters should wish to congregate together, not because of a common experience of exclusion but because they believed 'that cultural differences were genetically transmitted and only had their full impact in early adulthood' (Ibid., p. 70). But what are the policy implications of these perceptions?

In 1967 the report by Lord Hunt on *Immigrants and the Youth Service* had argued the case for an urgent attempt to integrate black youth by promoting multi-racial youth clubs (Hunt, 1967). By the early 1970s, it became apparent that separate provision would have to be accepted as a staging post to this eventual destination (YSIC, 1972). But the stimulus was the same; urgent action was necessary to prevent the race riots that had disfigured many major cities of North America.

The Commission for Racial Equality (CRE), anticipating the riots in Bristol in May 1980, has recently added its voice to those pressing for a coherent and immediate response at both national and local level. The CRE commends this statement from the Lambeth Inner City Partnership: 'The needs of young blacks, however manifested – particularly in unemployment, homelessness and crime figures – are a particular cause of concern (CRE, 1980c, p. 67). They go on to advocate that the solution lies in a comprehensive policy co-ordinated at the local level by a central youth unit with as many black advisers and staff members as possible.

The problem is defined as one where West Indian young people are likely to be heavily over-represented in the 'at risk' and 'alienated' categories of youth. The implication of this state of affairs is that special provision in the form of 'drop-in' centres, voluntary schemes and, above all, 'self-help' exercises should be mounted to cope with the presenting symptoms of this deep-seated malaise. As the CRE report warns:

The problem of youth in our inner cities, and particularly of ethnic minority youth, must be seen as a major issue for public policy. Disenchantment with society, leading to alienation, is becoming commonplace. Unless these trends are abated, society could experience serious strife in the eighties. (CRE, 1980c, p. 74)

At the central government level, the CRE concludes that nothing short of a special minister is called for to co-ordinate the expenditure of new funds in an increasingly black welfare service.

We have moved, then, from research data which suggests that West Indian young people occupy no special or particular role, but have their place in a complex and interdependent matrix of kin, to an official response which is urging institutionalised provision to cope with the 'problem' of black youth. There is no doubt that 'youth' has now become a problem; the only uncertainty is whether the reasons for this lie in some transformation that has so far escaped the attention of social anthropologists or whether it has been discovered by those whose professional skills may be brought to bear upon it. Now that it exists, it delineates a group that are seen as being in quite desperate straits. Young blacks are 'alienated', whereas their parents are not; they are unemployed, unhoused and uncouth. It is to the social services and the youth service that we must look to overcome this marginality.

The same general process can be found in the growing concern for the 'special needs' of black children. This springs from the realisation that a disproportionate number of children of Wst Indian descent are in the care of local authorities. A study in 1971 (before the full impact of the 1969 Children and Young Persons Act had occurred) found that 32 per cent of girls and 52 per cent of boys in approved schools (now community homes with education) in London and the south-east were from ethnic minorities (Harris, 1971). A further analysis of these data with some additional information gathered on the reasons for committal to approved school, or subsequently to a care order, found that the boys, in particular, were far less delinquent (as measured by the severity of offence at committal) than their white peers (Cawson, 1977).

As before, the official reaction to this fact has been to advocate the development of a black social service; the employment of more black social workers, child care officers and foster parents (HC, 1976–7, 180–1, para. 53). The danger is, of course, that a black youth service or social service may serve to confirm and not to deny the marginality from which black children and young people suffer. If the aetiology of a social problem is understood as cultural and if it is thought to require welfare intervention then that culture itself becomes flawed and race becomes compounded as a disability. The increasing employment of racial minorities themselves because they understand the culture only serves to legitimate this explanation.

(2) *Educational Marginality*

If there is one other area that has received massive attention, it is education. However, much of this has been to point out that ethnic minority children, and particularly young blacks, perform less well on certain tests of measured ability and appear to achieve less passes in examinations than their white peers. The truth of this matter remains unclear although a recent review of thirty-three studies – ranging from large-scale group tests to small-scale individual tests – found that in twenty-five instances average scores were indeed lower (Tomlinson, 1980).

Of course, achievement scores are also strongly class correlated and it matters perhaps more what reaction there has been to this understanding than to the fact itself. In general, there has been a readiness to accept the evidence and to respond with alacrity to the proposition that West Indian descended children have 'special needs'. This appreciation in general – that 'special needs' are central to service delivery – has recently been well expressed by the Home Office:

> Discrimination apart, any improvement in the situation depends also on a recognition, throughout the administration of the various services at both local and national level, that account has to be taken of the special needs and background of ethnic minority communities if they are to benefit from these services to the same extent as the rest of the population. (HC, 1979–80, 610–ii, para. 4)

Apart from the traditional Urban Programme, much of which was expanded on provision for the under-5s, the most important instance of this policy is, of course, the grants given under Section 11 of the 1966 Local Government Act which empowers the secretary of state to support local authorities who are required to make special provision for ethnic minorities from the New Commonwealth. Despite a recent review of this provision, to cope with the fact that such a high proportion of blacks and Asians are not immigrants and to allow expenditure on non-staff areas, the general commitment – which currently allows a 75 per cent grant unrelated to the calculation of the rate support allocation – will continue. Given the broad terms in which Section 11 is expressed, it is striking that so much of it has been used for educational expenditure as Table 3.1 shows.

What is remarkable is the degree to which this expenditure is concentrated on education, an area of concern which readily accords with the supposition that cultural differences, newness and unfamiliarity are the real enemies to be counteracted. In their review of the problems facing the 'West Indian community' in 1977 the Select Committee on Race Relations and Immigration laid considerable store by the need for an independent inquiry into the 'causes of the under-achievement of children of West

Table 3.1 *Allocations under Section 11 of the Local Government Act 1966 (1978/9) (per cent)*

Education and ancillary staff	85·1
Child-care staff	6·2
Day-nursery staff	2·1
Social workers	1·7
Environmental health officers	0·8
Liaison officers	0·4
Interpreters	0·2
Other staff	3·5
	100.0
	(£38·62 million)

Source: HC, 1979–80, 610–vii.

Note: Since 1967 £233 million has been spent under Section 11 and it remains one of the central planks of current policy and one of very few that are directly focused on ethnic minorities.

Indian origin', and it was this, together with the presumed over-representation of black children in the schools intended for those deemed educationally subnormal, that has received the most immediate response. By 1978 the government had published a report on 'special educational needs' (DES, 1978), which was particularly concerned with black children and the ESN schools and in March 1979 the committee under Mr Anthony Rampton was appointed to consider the progress of ethnic-minority children in schools and also 'whether their special needs are being met by the education system' (HC, 1979–80, 610–v).

There is, then, an emerging consensus that in certain areas the major problem to be addressed is not that of discrimination but that of 'disadvantage' giving rise to 'special needs'. It is manifest in the terms of reference of the 1979–80 Select Committee and is defined in a way which makes it quite clear that 'disadvantage' is nothing to do with racism. Mr Alex Lyon, for example, defines it in these terms: 'It is the fact that somebody does not speak the language, comes from a different cultural background and just because of that is disadvantaged in competing with people who live in this community.' This definition was prompted by what this member of the Select Committee saw as the 'wet liberalism' of the CRE who appeared to be reluctant to apportion the responsibility for disadvantage where it belonged: 'It is simply the desire not to be insensitive to the black minority groups by saying that there is something different about them which they ought to be able to overcome with a bit of help from the State' (HC, 1979–80, 610–vii, para. 701). Thus discrimination is an act perpetrated on a victim; 'disadvantage' is a malady caused by difference from, or non-acceptance of, 'British' culture.

Once again, therefore, the traumas associated with life in Britain are identified as cultural phenomena. It is not simply that the consequences of racism become transmuted into the practice of 'normal' culture, but that this culture itself is seen as deficient and flawed. An example from the realm of child-rearing may serve to illustrate this point. The anthropology of West Indian societies makes frequent mention of the strength and closeness of the mother–child bond. Edith Clarke's famous study of Jamaica concludes: 'They are continually together. The woman depends on even very young children to fetch and carry for her. Whatever she may be doing in the yard, the children are never very far away. There is constant companionship, and a constant inter-dependence (Clarke, 1966, p. 158).

It is a long way, indeed, from this appreciation to that of Mr Anthony Steen, a past member of the Select Committee on Race Relations and Immigration who identifies the 'problem' of West Indian child care in these terms: 'The West Indian cultural pattern fails to perceive the benefits that accrue from playing and talking with children (HC, 1976–7, 180–1, p. 61). With that kind of deficiency it is no wonder that the black British have been seen to have 'special needs'.

I shall now look at two areas where 'special needs' are not so readily identified. It is important to note that if special attention was required here it would be less easy to deny positive discrimination in the allocation of resources.

(3) *Locational Marginality*

It is commonly accepted that Britain's black population came to rest in the so-called 'twilight zones' around the centres of major cities, in particular London and Birmingham (Rex and Moore, 1967). As a result of that location, they are thought to be the direct and evident beneficiaries of areal policies developed to combat the housing and environmental conditions that are now seen as the hallmark of 'inner-city' residents. We have to ask, therefore, whether this well-known pattern is still extant and, further, whether the areal policies of positive discrimination are likely to come to grips with the poor conditions that it portends.

The evidence that we have to go on is defective and inadequate. What there is, however, suggests a massive change of housing tenure for the West Indian descended population from the boarding-houses of the twilight zones to local authority housing, much of it outside the confines of the 'inner city' as defined by the areas of the Inner City Partnerships. The main evidence comes from the *National Dwelling and Housing Survey, 1977/8* (DoE, 1979) which employed the Partnership zones to define the 'inner city'. In Manchester, Birmingham and London, 'West Indians' are still between two and three times as likely to live in the inner city, but all minority groups together only account for 17 per cent of the total inner-city population (HC, 1979–80, 610–vi) however, the West Indian population is now no more likely than any other group to live in multiple occupancy, although they are still more likely to experience overcrowding (Cross and Johnson, 1980; Johnson, Cross and Parker, 1981).

What is important is that the black population, whether inner or outer city, is more likely than any other group to be occupying local authority housing (Table 3.2).

Table 3.2   *Proportion of Households in Local Authority Housing by Race, 1977/8 (per cent)*

| Racial Group | City | | | |
| | London | | Birmingham | |
	Inner	Outer	Inner	Outer
White	55·3	28·9	37·4	37·8
West Indian	60·9	42·3	37·9	47·5
Indian	32·6	11·6	3·3	13·1
Pakistani/Bangladeshi	33·8	22·1	7·6	(0)
Other	44·4	19·4	8·6	20·4
All	54·5	28·4	32·6	37·4
(N)	(14,297)	(143,848)	(1,351)	(4,413)

Source: *National Dwelling and Housing Survey, 1977/8* (DoE, 1979).

While it may be desirable that the black population penetrated the local authority tenure to such an extent, by the same token it must, therefore, mean that schemes to improve the other housing stock must have less relevance. At the end of 1979 there were 436 Housing Action Areas and 40 per cent were in areas where minorities made up 10 per cent or more of the population. But since Housing Action Areas are not intended to improve local authority stock they are more likely to benefit those groups with low levels of local authority tenure (HC, 1979–80, 610–vi).

The main component of social policy concerned with the inner cities is, of course, the Urban Programme. To what extent does this represent a concerted attempt to redress racial injustice? In the early period, as Edwards and Batley (1978) have pointed out, the Urban Programme was based on a social pathology theory of urban deprivation that identified the proportion of blacks as a clear symptom of malaise. The White Paper of 1977 and the Inner Urban Areas Act of 1978 demonstrated a major shift of thinking that now embraced the theory that inner-city problems were the result of failing local economies. Under the Labour government the solution to these questions was perceived as lying in a new comprehensive policy of local and central government co-operation in which a concerted attempt would be made to stimulate economic and environmental regeneration. The change of government in May 1979 saw a further gloss on this policy which now includes a much greater emphasis on individual entre-preneurship and much less on comprehensive planning.

There are four elements to the current Urban Programme in which the seven Partnerships are by far the most important. The other three include fifteen Programme Authorities each of which receive between £2 million to £3·5 million each, fourteen other authorities who receive much less and the traditional Urban Programme, based on bids for 75 per cent funding, which cur-rently includes a further 120 authorities. It is clear from Table 3.3 that the seven Partnerships receive the lion's share of the available funds (currently £192 million).

Table 3.3   *Allocation of Urban Programme Funds 1980/1 (per cent)*

Partnership Authorities (7)	58
Programme Authorities (15)	22
Other Authorities (14)	3
Traditional Urban Programme (120)	17
	100
	(£192 million)

Source: HC, 1979–80, 610–vi.

There are at least three ways in which the expenditure of these funds cannot now be said to constitute positive discrimination in favour of the black population.

In the first place 62 per cent of the ethnic-minority population does not live in the areas covered by either the Partnerships or the Programme Authorities (HC, 1979–80, 610–vi). Secondly, there is no correlation between the proportion of minority popula-tion in a Partnership Authority and the allocation of funds to that authority. This is evident from Table 3.4 which gives the per capita allocation to the seven Partnerships and the proportion of the population which is comprised of ethnic minorities.

Table 3.4   *Per Capita Allocations in the Inner-City Partnerships 1980–1*

Partnership Authority	Per Capita Allocation (£)	Minority Population (per cent)
Birmingham	63·44	6·4
London (Lambeth)	50·00	27·5
London (Hackney/Islington)	37·43	23·3
London (Docklands)	529·85	13·0
Manchester/Salford	54·84	10·7
Liverpool	62·37	3·6
Newcastle/Gateshead	64·57	2·0

Source: HC, 1979–80, 610–vi.

Even leaving aside the extraordinary allocation to the docklands project, there is no significant difference between the per capita allocations to Birmingham and Liverpool, even though the inner-city zone of the former has a minority presence ten times as great as the latter. On the assumption that the allocations benefit all citizens equally, the minorities receive only 15·7 per cent of the aggregate per capita allocations while comprising 17·1 per cent of the population of the Parnership areas. This is very much in line with the 1977 White Paper which specifically rejects positive discrimination on racial or ethnic lines (DoE, 1977).

Thirdly, there is the evidence on the distribution of Urban Programme money for projects which are specifically designed for ethnic minorities. A review by the Department of the Environment in January 1980 concluded that 18 per cent of total allocations went on ethnic-minority projects, which appears on the high side since only approximately 10 per cent of funds find their way to the voluntary sector of the Partnership and it is here, in the traditional Urban Programme, that the majority of minority projects are funded (HC, 1979–80, 610–vi). A particular case may illustrate the general point: the Birmingham Partnership Area has the highest proportion from the ethnic minorities so that we might expect them to fare particularly well in the allocation of resources if a policy of positive discrimination was being pursued. In fact, ethnic-minority organisations, or those with projects specifically designed to aid ethnic minorities, did apply for a third of the available funds in 1980–1, which is roughly in accord with the demographic composition of the Partnership area. However, they received only 13 per cent of the funds. The average grants approved for minority or multi-cultural organisations was

£7,000 but for white organisations it was £17,000 (Birmingham CRC, 1980). Overall, ethnic-minority organisations received only 3·9 per cent of what they asked for, compared with 20·6 per cent for other groups. Multi-cultural organisations fared better, receiving 16 per cent of their requests. In other words ethnic minorities were just as likely to apply for money under the Urban Programme in Birmingham, but they were less likely to be successful than white groups and when they were successful they received, on average, allocations less than half as much, which was not due to the size of their original submissions (Birmingham CRC, 1980). If this is replicated elsewhere it is evident that the traditional Urban Programme does not represent anything approximating to positive discrimination.

As far as black youth is concerned there is no evidence to suggest that current policy represents a systematic attempt at overcoming the peripheral location of young blacks in the urban system. That would require the allocation of resources in ways which could be seen to affect blacks positively in relation to whites and no such evidence can be adduced. Marginality is manufactured by default as a policy which is less relevant for one group than others must widen the gap between the two.

(4)   *Occupational Marginality*

It is well known that the occupational distribution of the West Indian descended population is heavily skewed to manual work. The National Dwelling and Housing Survey found that only 16·3 per cent of black household heads were in non-manual work with twice that proportion in white households. However, it is wrong to assume that black workers are unskilled for 61 per cent are in semi-skilled or skilled work compared with 43 per cent of workers overall (HC, 1979–80, 610–vii).

Unemployment amongst black household heads at the time of the *National Dwelling and Housing Survey* (DoE, 1979) was 9·7 per cent compared with 3·5 per cent nationally. As Table 3.5 shows, as far as London and Birmingham are concerned, the relative position of black households is worse in the outer city than the inner. That is, black households appear to carry their higher risk of unemployment to the non-Partnership areas, whereas other groups are less likely to do so.

As far as young people are concerned the position is far worse than these figures suggest. Table 3.6 is based on the same survey and it shows that, taken nationally, UK-born blacks (defined as of West Indian descent) suffered unemployment at four or five times the rate of the white population (HC, 1979–80, 610–iv). Of course,

Table 3.5 *Proportion of Household Heads Unemployed* (per cent)*

| Racial Group | London | | Birmingham | |
	Inner	Outer	Inner	Outer
White	5·6	2·5	6·6	4·0
West Indian	9·5	7·1	14·3	15·4
Indian	7·0	3·0	11·9	5·4
uPakistani/Bangladeshi	12·9	5·6	6·6	(11·1)
Other	7·8	4·1	(10·5)	5·5
Total	6·3	2·8	8·2	4·2

Source: National Dwelling and Housing Survey 1977/8 (DoE, 1979).
* Those seeking work as proportions of those in labour market.

four out of five UK-born blacks are under 30 years of age so we are
seeing both an age and race effect.

Young blacks are particularly prone on both counts. A rise in
the unemployment rate for all males of 1 per cent is accompanied
by a rise in the rate for males under 20 of 1·7 per cent (Makeham,
1980). Moreover, between March 1979 and February 1980 the
official figures record 2·5 per cent rise in unemployment and an
11·6 per cent rise in unemployment amongst ethnic minorities
(HC, 1979–80, 610–iv). The latter jump cannot be fully accounted
for by the overall age effect. Thus, in times of recession, age and
race have a compound negative effect on our unemployment
prospects. It is worth restating that the differences in educational
or job qualifications do not account for the low earnings and job
levels of minorities, while on unemployment recent survey data
were consistent with the hypothesis that 'Asians and West
Indians experience lengthy unemployment to some extent
because they are black, regardless of their occupational level,
earnings and state of health' (Smith, 1980, p. 604).

It is also worth noting that the *relatively* poor position of the
young black unemployed is not confined to the lower echelons of
the employment structure. In fact, if the *National Dwelling and
Housing Survey* data are any guide, the opposite is true: the ratio
of non-white to white unemployment rates is highest for young
people with non-manual and skilled manual occupations even

Table 3.6 *Unemployment Rates by Sex and Race 1977/8 (per cent)*

| Birthplace | Black | | White | |
	Male	Female	Male	Female
UK-born	21·0	24·0	5·3	4·6
Non-UK-born	9·2	7·5	—	—

Source: National Dwelling and Housing Survey 1977/8 (DoE, 1979).

though the unskilled, from whatever race, suffer higher levels of unemployment.

In these circumstances one is looking to social policy for clear and positive attempts to counteract and overcome the effects of racism in recruitment, promotion and levels of remuneration. As far as the recruitment across the board is concerned the most obvious plank of policy is to be found in the 1976 Race Relations Act. There is not the space for review of the employment implications of this legislation, although it is hard to conclude that it can have had more than a marginal effect. For example, there were 426 employment complaints to industrial tribunals under the At in the year ending 30 June 1980. In only 5·2 per cent cases was the complaint upheld; 40·6 per cent were withdrawn and 42·4 per cent were dismissed (DE, 1980).

The policy on individual discrimination is not, in fact, the main focus of attention for the problems faced by black youth. It is to the Manpower Services Commission (MSC) that we have to turn and, in particular, to the massive resources now channelled into the Special Programmes Division for the financing of the Youth Opportunity Programme (YOP). The theory underlying this programme is reasonably clear. It is that unemployment amongst young people is exacerbated – if not caused – by inappropriate attitudes to work and a lack of appropriate skills. The answer is perceived to lie in a complex package of schemes for 16–19-year-olds divided into those that are loosely described as 'work preparation' and those that provide various forms of work experience. In 1979/80 the 216,000 entrants on schemes costing £115·6 million were divided as in Table 3.7.

Table 3.7   *Distribution of YOP Entrants by Scheme Type 1979/80 (per cent)*

Work Preparation	
Employment induction courses	1·4
Short training courses	13·5
Remedial courses	1·0
Work Experience	
Work experience on employers' premises	64·2
Project-based work experience	7·0
Training workshops	3·4
Community service	9·5
	100·0
	(216,400)

Source: MSC, 1980, p. 11.

It is apparent, therefore that the vast majority of places are provided on short training courses, usually of thirteen weeks' duration at colleges of further education, or in 'work experience on employers' premises' which last on average twenty-two weeks.

It is too early to provide a research-based conclusion on the impact of YOP schemes on the young black school-leaver. However, there are three areas of general concern. First, there is the question of training itself. At many places the original rationale for the YOP makes it seem as if the provision is going to be for vocational training. For example, the original press release in February 1978 quoted a speech by the present chairman of the MSC, Sir Richard O'Brien, in which he said: 'We know that many young people simply do not possess the skills, knowledge and kinds of experience employers will be looking for. New jobs will require more skills not less' (MSC, 1978, p. 6). Moreover, the feasibility study by Geoffrey Holland speaks of 'unified vocational preparation' and argues forcefully that: 'Each component of the new programme must therefore be designed to enable the individual to do more things, achieve a higher level of skills, knowledge and performance and adapt more readily to changing circumstances or job requirements' (MSC, 1977, p. 34). While it is true that elsewhere the schemes are described in less grandiose terms as a 'constructive alternative to unemployment' one might be forgiven for supposing that young people would receive training in specific skills that would enable them to fill vacancies in skilled employment.

As far as black youngsters are concerned such courses would be welcomed. We have powerful independent evidence that recruitment to apprentices operates systematically against young members of minority groups (Lee and Wrench, 1980). The supply of craft apprenticeships and training courses provided by employers rarely meets the demand. In these circumstances, a pronounced tendency for firms to employ the 'lads of dads' through an informal network of contact and information militates against the just recruitment of black youth. Black youngsters are forced to depend more on the careers service which is regarded by employers as an inferior source of apprenticeships and trainees (ibid., p. 108).

The MSC provision may compound this problem since it provides what at first sight appears to be vocational training but which is not. (Or at least is only incidentally so. The employment of skilled men as supervisors inevitably means that some understanding of basic technique is imparted but this is not seen in the MSC as the main purpose of the enterprise and it rarely lasts long enough to have much cumulative impact.) The result is that many young people express dissatisfaction with what they have received and there is a real danger that participation in such schemes underlines rather than undermines the categorisation of black youth as unemployable or as second-rate. As Howard Williamson recently concluded 'the label "unemployable" is being attached increasingly to YOP trainees, with the implication that certain personal characteristics (such as laziness, or non-acceptance of discipline) must be corrected before they have any chance of securing a "real" job' (Williamson, 1980, p. 6). There is widespread acceptance within the MSC that special provision is required for minority youth (MSC, 1979) but if that provision acts to confirm rather than to destroy the racist image of black youth as less desirable than white it will hardly have helped its clients.

Even if we accept that MSC provision is, on balance, beneficial, there is evidence that some programmes of particular relevance have been reduced. For example, black youths tend to leave school later than their white peers so that they are more likely to be in need of work at a later age. Yet it is precisely the Special Temporary Employment Programme (STEP) (originally announced to run in parallel with YOP), which is specifically designed to provide work for those aged 19 to 24 years, unemployed for at least six months that has been cut back. The scheme now operates with only a third as many places as originally intended in the Special Development Areas, the Development Areas and certain inner-city zones. Even the MSC was moved to comment that 'the relative burden of unemployment in the minorities falls on those aged 19 and over. Here, particularly following the reduction in STEP, there is a sizeable gap between needs and provision' (HC, 1979–80, 610–iv, para. 4.9).

There is little evidence, therefore, that current employment policy provides positive discrimination in favour of black young people. Once again, there is a growing awareness of 'special needs' but these are seen as more for remedial courses or remedial education than for increased access to employment. One example of the latter is the growing interest in the provision of 'social and life skills' training which has been justly criticised as another form of 'compensatory education' with its well-known capacity to redirect attention away from structural position to the failings of individuals, in this case of unemployed young people (Atkinson *et al.*, 1980).

Conclusion

Commentators on the evidence of continuing discrimination tend to argue either that we need to do more of what we are already doing or that we need to rethink the whole approach, laying emphasis more on the processes of discrimination than its victims. The radical tenor of the second thesis is appealing as there are few grounds for optimism with the current situation. However, the conclusion that no attention should be given to the victims of discrimination is overly hasty; what matters is the precise form that this attention takes. In any case, the argument that elements of current policy simply 'blame the victim' is too easy to refute. It is not the 'blaming' of the victim which is frequently evident but the apportioning of responsibility for his problems to his culture or customs. He can hardly be held personally culpable for his culture but, nevertheless, it is to the change of that culture or custom that policy is directed.

A outsider to policies on race relations might be struck by two, apparently contradictory, elements. On the one hand, there is a great deal of attention given to some topics and, on the other, very little given to those that could be seen to discriminate negatively against the white population. Unlike the policies pursued in the USA, the observer would note that problems of school-level achievement or of youth itself appear to take precedence over policies of positive discrimination in employment. In the former case, there appears to be an enthusiasm to compensate for the deficiencies of the groups identified as requiring attention. In the latter, what is striking is a lack of willingness to admit the need for special provision unless somehow the problem can be redefined as one requiring compensation. If one is to argue that policies, on the whole, have magnified or manufactured marginality then it is necessary to criticise both approaches. I shall call the first 'negative compensation' and the second 'positive non-discrimination' to indicate the possible difficulties with the intervention in some cases and its studious avoidance in others. More precisely we may define these concepts as:

Negative compensation – the identification of a group for special attention in ways which detract from rather than advance the interests of its members.

Positive non-discrimination – the refusal to identify a group for special attention when the interests of its members may be served by doing so.

Of course, it is easy to overstate this case. It is unlikely that all compensatory policies are negative in their effects and it is possible to point to some cases where discrimination has indeed favoured minorities. On balance, however, the effects of social policy on black youth do not appear to be lessening the tensions or ameliorating the hurts of racism. In particular, they do not appear to have confronted racism itself.

The argument in this chapter has been descriptive and not explanatory. If it has worth, then we require to know why policies have been so minimal in positive impact. The answer to that is itself complex, deriving from an interaction of political constraints, economic imperatives and, above all, a peculiar history that permits common-sense theories of cultural deficiency to gain credence as incontravertible truth. In consequence, the second-class citizenship of black youth can be made to seem inevitable if not unproblematic. Of course, black youngsters will not accept these explanations although whether they have the power to de-label themselves *and* to successfully direct attention to white racism remains to be seen.

4 West Indian and Asian Youth

JOHN REX

It is almost a platitude in race-relations research in Britain today to say that the host–mmigrant framework is not appropriate and that we have to recognise that immigrants enter a conflictual and class-divided society. Little attention has been given, however, to the implications of this statement for the other mode of entry to the society through socialisation rather than physical immigration. The child of immigrant parents does not merely have to be socialised into some seamless British culture. He enters into a complex process of intergenerational and class conflict in which he will both share experiences with working-class and middle-class British youth and be divided from them.

All industrial societies, of course, produce intergenerational conflict and youth counter-cultures. The basis for this lies in the fact that, given the impersonal nature of adult society and of work roles in the industrial (capitalist or communist) system, children must first be socialised into the family and then out of it. One of the most interesting contributions of Talcott Parsons to theoretical and empirical sociology has been his extension of a basically psychoanalytic approach to these problems, from the traumas of the first five years of life to the traumas of adolescence (Parsons, 1949, ch. 9).

Parsons suggests that socialisation out of the family necessarily involves strain in that the child, having been socialised into a *Gemeinschaft* system of roles characterised by affectivity, diffuseness, particularism, ascription and collectivity orientation, is now required to move towards roles in the *Gesellschaft*, characterised by affective neutrality, specificity, universalism, achievement-orientation and self-orientation. The conflicting demands of this situation produce an ambivalence which can only be resolved by suppressing one set of demands by a doubly intensive and 'compulsive' pursuit of the other. For boys this means rejecting the apron strings of the family role system and behaving in an apparently callous and aggressive masculine way. For girls there is a more complex reaction which, according to Parsons, turns upon the nature of the adult female role as wife-mother and upon the fact that access to that role involves finding a partner among the compulsively masculine male adolescents, through differentiation of herself as sexy from the soft and gentle appeal of the boy's mother.

Peer-group cultures and societies, according to Parsons, both sustain the compulsive masculinity and its female equivalent in adolescent culture and then, by providing security for adolescents and members, serve eventually to eliminate anxiety which makes the compulsiveness necessary. The social system of the school serves, according to another of Parsons's essays (1961) to ease this transition. It actually rewards social success in the peer-group culture but in conjunction with achievement in the more respectable achievement system of the school. Peer-group culture thus becomes domesticated and unthreatening.

The traumas of adolescence are inevitable and Parsons has made an important contribution by emphasising them independently of the 'first five years of life' which are too often given primacy amongst those who write in the psychoanalytic tradition. It must be assumed that these traumas impose problems in their own right, that social systems have ways of handling those problems, and that they are sometimes unsuccessful, producing deviance and sustained intergenerational conflict.

In fact, however, Parsons does not develop his ideas about adolescent traumas and intergenerational conflict and deviance independently of the first five years of life. He deals with the mechanisms for handling and controlling the threatening subculture but does not say what he believes will happen if that subculture gets out of hand (1952). Rather he deals with deviance and social control as a topic not specifically in relation to the first five years of life or of adolescence but as a feature of learning situations in the abstract. The role-players in learning situations, described as 'socialiser' and 'socialisee' are in a situation of emotional dependence which is threatened by the fact that the socialiser, by the nature of his teaching role, seeks to elicit new behaviours and extinguish old ones. This betrayal of expectations leads to ambivalence and to a variety of compulsive ways of handling it, unless certain 'adequacies' exist in the learning situation. It is assumed that a majority of socialisees actually do learn adequately without strain, ambivalence and compulsiveness, but that, whether in early socialisation or in adolescence, there will be casualties and that these casualties will act out their compulsive patterns in any situation of social interaction with which they are confronted. There will also arise social groups and subcultures at all points which sustain compulsiveness and deviance.

Parsons thus gives us two theories: a theory of adolescent socialisation and subcultures and a theory of the genesis, development and control of deviance. One would have to note that the second theory needed to be applied to the former in order to produce a theory of deviance and conflict amongst adolescents.

In seeking to apply Parsons's theories to British adolescents, British youth culture and British schools, one cannot but notice that, compared with the empirical reality, Parsons appears to deal with a strange, classless world. It is therefore important to notice that, within the British socialisation and educational system, the very mechanisms which Parsons describes operate in an idiom of class and that class cultures and class conflict add a whole new dimension to the problems with which he deals. Even more is it the case that the socialisation of children from immigrant minorities raises problems of a political sort.

The British educational system centres around themes of class, status and mobility to a degree which is probably unparalleled anywhere else in the world. In fact it can be argued that, however much sociologists may seek to make analytic distinctions between class status and power, the very focus of the debate about 'class' in a loose sense is to be found in the school system. In trying to disentangle the problems faced by the children of immigrants in entering the British social system, therefore, this is where we have to begin.

Official ideologies of education in Britain place primary emphasis upon the task of selection in discovering and educating the intellectually gifted child, while at the same time providing for the majority an education appropriate to their condition and separating out the 'remedials' with a view either to restoring them to the mainstream or keeping them out of the system so that they do not constitute a nuisance. The important sociological questions to be asked about such ideologies, however, (and it is not simply asked out of class envy or cynicism) is whether the intellectual qualities on which the whole system is thought to turn are not in fact social qualities. Certainly this is my own view. From Oxford and Cambridge down through the public schools and the grammar schools to the higher streams in comprehensive schools, children are being selected out who will break their ties with their peers, will develop new commitments to membership of a solidary élite which despises the mass and the mob, and will value, above all, individual achievement both in skills and knowledge and in the acquisition of élite culture. Selective education in the state sector was once the key to this and the grammar school was the means whereby the main selection of working-class children for promotion was made. A recurrent theme in biography and in literature has been that of the 'missionary' teacher who, while teaching in a poor, working-class environment, finds a gifted child whom he or she then sponsors and encourages to pursue an academic career leading eventually to an Oxford or Cambridge scholarship.

The grammar school provided a secure environment for this process of sponsorship, separation and socialisation to occur. It also involved the prolongation of adolescence and the control and utilisation of peer-group culture through sport, which is, in fact, very similar to what Parsons described in his 'The school class as a social system' (1961). The culture of such schools was centred around non-utilitarian subjects and the games played were élite games which were readily distinguished from those popular amongst the population at large. Language came to be used in a new way and emotions subject to a kind of code of gentility and restraint quite unlike that in working-class life as such (see Bernstein, 1961).

Missionary processes like this, however, could not and did not assume that working-class children selected for promotion were totally malleable. The children had to be saved from working-class culture, from peer-group culture and from working-class youth culture. This meant that there were real pressures restricting mobility and that nothing which was done to reward mobility success, actually eliminated as a social reality another culture distinct from that which the school system was designed to promote.

The culture of resistance which existed in the lower streams and institutions of the school system is not to be thought of in negative terms as simply being characterised by a lack of grammar-school qualities. It included many of the elements of the peer-group culture which Parsons describes and was rewarding for the children in that it enabled them to explore immediately and compulsively the more adult roles which the prolonged adolescence of the grammar schools disallowed. Children claimed the right to grow up more quickly and they despised the childish goody-goodiness of the grammar school. They also had the strong and comfortable sense of belonging to the majority. If the language which they used lacked the discrimination and subtlety of that which prevailed in the grammar schools it had rewarding meanings in terms of reinforcing social bonds. Emotions were not tightly disciplined and organised so as to facilitate easy and genteel social intercourse of the upper-class sort but, by way of contrast, allowed for the strong expression of love and hate and for broad undifferentiated social solidarity. Popular arts and popular sports served to symbolise this cultural-emotional situation and the more that the authorities sought to suppress and control the expressions which surrounded these activities, the more they appealed as a kind of ecstatic release. If the keynote of upper-class emotion and culture was restraint it was this quality of carnival and ecstasy which characterised the culture of the masses (Bell, 1977).

Popular culture produced an alternative world for youth. The young men who became professional footballers had little in the way of education, yet they performed their arts before crowds greater than could be gathered together for any other occasion. Similarly, the young musicians whose records sold millions or who performed before vast rock festivals positively gloried in their rejection of school values. From the point of view of the missionary schoolteachers and their converts this culture was a form of escape. To those who participated in it, it was the reality which the po-faced disciplines of the school prevented the scholarship children from understanding. In fact, of course, even such children came to retain links with this cultural package, dipping into the sea of ecstasy in a controlled way in order to sustain themselves with the life which their disciplines denied.

The threatening nature of the ecstatic working-class youth subculture meant that it had to be rigorously segregated and controlled. A bi-partite or tri-partite education system was one way of doing this. In the grammar school, boys played rugby, girls hockey, and musical appreciation and individual performance in classical music and with classical instruments were encouraged. The secondary-modern schools were run with a view to controlling elements of a culture which could not be repressed and perhaps allowing a few to actually win a few grammar-school-type awards. Outside the schools, the police came to regard almost as their major activity the shepherding, controlling and at times the harassing of the young people who paraded in support of their football teams or their musical idols. Most accepted that the police had a right to confine their activities and the police were forced to learn a measure of tolerance. But, on the margins, there were those who burst the bounds, who performed impermissible acts or who actually resisted the imposition of authority. They came to be called hooligans and vandals.

Relatively recently, of course, pressure from parents anxious that the tri-partite system endangered their children's chances led to the elimination of grammar schools from the system. Missionary work and sponsorship now had to take place within the comprehensive school and with far less opportunity to segregate those who were being sponsored for mobility. The solidary ecstatic and anti-academic working-class youth culture was there on the spot as eternal temptation to the gifted and the sponsored to backslide. This could mean, and perhaps in the long run it will mean, a reintegration of culture, of individual achievement and group solidarity, of discipline and ecstasy. For the moment, however, the lines of battle are very sharply drawn and a minority of working-class children who are on the verge of sponsorship face a dreadful either/or.

For English working-class children, however, their situation under the old tri-partite dispensation or the new comprehensive one is not all that unacceptable. However much a child may be by-passed in the sponsorship process, he or she still has an acceptable destiny when he/she leaves school. He or she has the opportunity of entering his or her parents' world. The parents provide the contacts and entry may be obtained to a secure industrial job. There, school education may matter little. On-the-job training leads to the acquisition of skills and even to promotion and, in any case, in many jobs trade-union protection guarantees that the young worker is treated with dignity. Moreover, at home there are supports to be found and roles to be played in communal working-class life. All this adds up to a significant social wage and, even though for many parents seeing their children enter the adult working class may appear only as a second best after the possibility of promotion to a white-collar or professional world has been lost, it is none the less not a way of life to be regretted and, so long as a powerful labour movement exists, one which will provide security in adult life.

This, then, is the system which the child of an immigrant must enter. It is obviously not a simple world, of a 'host society.' The questions are: Can the immigrant child go straight into and up the system and share in the educational success of the sponsored English child? If he cannot do this, will he be able to enter fully into the non-sponsored life of the working class? If he cannot do either of these things what will his position be? Will he belong to a third culture beneath or to the side of the class system we have described? What will be the cultural idiom in terms of which his situation is expressed? Will the relationship between any immigrant minority culture and that of British class culture be one of symbiosis, of conflict, or of a relatively uneasy truce?

There is not a single answer to these questions because in Britain there is no single immigrant minority. There are a number of white minorities who are rarely even discussed as immigrants and there are also two very visible groups of dark-skinned minorities from the Caribbean and from the Indian subcontinent, amongst whom there are many regional and class subtypes. The young West Indian male expressing himself on the street through the symbolism of Ras Tafari is all too often taken to be the sole or typical representative of 'immigrant' or 'black' youth as such. He is, of course, important, but there are a great many other possible immigrant situations and, in order to restore a more balanced perspective it is perhaps useful to begin elsewhere. This analysis therefore begins with the Asian and, so far as West Indian youth is concerned, looks at other social types as well as the young Rasta.

Some sort of cultural bi-lingualism is, as we have seen, an essential part of the situation of the English working-class child; that is to say that he is under pressure to live one kind of cultural life in the school and another type at home. For youth, at least, this contrast also takes the form of a contrast between repression and discipline, on the one hand, and ecstasy, on the other, even though the situation may be somewhat more complicated in that the ecstatic working-class youth culture also has to confront adult working-class puritanism. In any case, however, the first point to notice about Asian children is that their bi-lingual, bi-cultural situation is, in part, like that of the working-class native child and, in part, dissimilar from it.

There are working-class homes in which children are required to accept and support the class and regional values of the home while at the same time 'bi-lingually' adjusting to the middle class and national values of the school, because such instrumental acceptance of values is known to be important to economic success. Such families come closest to the families of Asian children.

Asian families, be they Sikh, Hindu or Muslim, Pakistani, Indian or Bangladeshi, are all, compared with English families, tight-knit and all attached more or less strongly to a culture pattern far more sharply differentiated from English culture than working-class English culture is differentiated from the middle-class culture of the schools. The child has very strong ties to quite specific kin, either in Britain or in the Indian subcontinent. Such ties imply duties and respect for authority which cannot be denied either through a child's affiliation to a permissive and ecstatic youth culture or through his being sponsored into middle-class success.

It is certainly not possible to see the culture of the Asian child's home as an ecstatic culture to be contrasted with the discipline of middle-class school culture. If anything, the disciplines of the family culture are more severe. There is undoubtedly an ecstatic element in this culture but it is at the service of its discipline rather than opposed to it. The problem, however, is that the children must now step outside of this well-integrated culture to perform well within another discipline seen as secular, utilitarian and instrumental. In this situation, the ecstatic working-class youth culture appears as doubly alien and dangerous. It is corrupting of family values and damaging to any prospects of instrumental success in the culture to which the immigrant has necessarily and seriously to adjust.

So far as I am aware, there have not been any Indian footballers or pop-stars, even though, as we shall see, there are many young West Indians to be found in both of these spheres. Indian boys and girls play those games which the school curriculum requires, just as they are encouraged to try to prove themselves so far as they are able in any academic tests which come their way. Their ambition will be to enter professional, white-collar or at least skilled manual occupations. Dirty factory- and foundry-work is seen as an undeniable feature of the immigrant situation not to be repeated in another generation. Some values derived from working-class experience in India and Britain will be transmitted to the next generation and Indians are more likely than any other group to vote Labour. None the less this will be coupled with a healthy respect for economic success and increase in the family's honour through individual success.

Emile Durkheim, in his classic study of suicide (1950), suggested that there were two types of social solidarity and three types of breakdown leading to suicide which were related to those types of solidarity. Altruistic solidarity required that the individual subordinate his whole life and interests to those of the group. Egoistic solidarity, although an apparent contradiction in terms, involved the subordination of the individual's interests and desires to an ego or conscience which, although autonomous and self-processing, was a social creation. The breakdown leading to altruistic suicide was one in which the demands of society and culture were so strong that they, in effect, destroyed the individual. The breakdown leading to egoistic suicide was one in which the individual accepted social norms but lacked the human support of another so that he eventually found his social isolation insupportable. A third type of breakdown was one in which the individual simply lived in a state of normlessness with no moral guideposts whatever and with no reason for, or for that matter against, living.

Most attempts to account for deviance tend to employ a model akin to Durkheim's third type of breakdown and it may be partially appropriate, as we shall see, to West Indian homeless and unemployed youth. It seems hardly appropriate in the case of Asian youth. Their situation is, first of all, one of altruistic solidarity. Girls are required to accept considerable limitations on their freedom of movement and, above all, to accept arranged marriages. Boys may be required to give their wages to their fathers and also to accept arranged marriages. For girls, marriage might occur while they are still at school. The majority of children born to Indian immigrants live within this system and may even feel themselves sustained by it. It should be noted that it brings rewards as well as imposing obligations. An arranged marriage with a considerable dowry has advantages over a 'romantic' one committed to penury.

In addition to such a life of altruistic solidarity, however, the Asian schoolchild is pressed into a competitive and individualistic world and is expected to do well there. The remarkable thing is that many fulfil their expectations even though they are subject simultaneously to the demands of altruistic and egoistic solidarity, having to achieve well *individually* for the sake of *family* honour. We must now see, however, what happens in cases of breakdown.

First, it should be noted that the family culture and values are under threat from two sources. On the one hand, the individualist middle-class culture is not fully in harmony with it, as it can be interpreted to mean a denial of family obligations and certainly has a place within it for marriage based on romantic love. On the other, there is the overwhelming threat of the ecstatic working-class culture, presenting as it does a world of eroticism outside the control of the family. There must be few Indian girls who have not been tempted by these possibilities, particularly as they are presented in popular music. Thus, being a good Indian and being a successful middle-class student at the same time are by no means easy goals to attain. There is bound to be breakdown.

Police claim that, whereas West Indian boys get into trouble because they are out of control, the problems presented by the Indian community are often those arising from violence in the enforcement of discipline or fighting for the control of institutions. From the point of view of Indian youth, what this means is that any possibility of deviance on their part will bring down the most violent oppression on them. The decision to deviate, therefore, is a very dramatic, even a cataclysmic one. Over and above all other punishments the individual becomes a moral outcast. The very intensity of social control ensures that there will be a small group of outcasts of this kind (see Rex and Tomlinson, 1979).

Inevitably, in the long run, the pressures of living in British society will mean that the altruistic pressures of Indian culture will abate and the adoption of English values, especially middle-class values, will become more frequent. It may well be a long time, however, before the Indian culture is so weakened, both externally and in the consciences of the young, that changed patterns, particularly of marriage, will be adopted without conflict. This will be particularly true amongst the low-caste, working-class majority who see the lifestyle of high-caste professional people, which has often become secularised to the extent of allowing inter-racial marriage, as too alien for comment.

In emphasising the likely style to be adopted by Indian deviants, however, we should not imagine that such deviance is widespread. What is perhaps more characteristic of the present is the extent to which young Indians assert their own culture. Of course, they encounter racism and the peculiar feature of the racism which is directed at them is that their culture is deemed to be inferior. A few may respond to this by shamefacedly abandoning it, but at least equally as powerful is an even more radical adherence to the culture. This is not exactly equivalent to the assertion of working-class culture in reaction to failure in the selective system. It might well go along with success in that system, but in reaction to racism which applies to the successful and the unsuccessful alike.

Asian young people have ready to hand a highly effective communal economic, social and political system to help them to cope with the exigencies of life in an alien land. Workers can turn to friends and kinsmen to help them into employment and can rely upon ethnic as well as trade-union solidarity in industrial disputes. Individuals buying houses can borrow from their kin. The extended family will mobilise capital to send a child to college, to buy entry to the professions or to start a business. Such an organisation is a powerful means of self-defence. Not surprisingly, therefore, the integration of Asians into British social and political organisations remains incomplete. Indians may join the Labour Party or trade unions but that is a secondary means of action. Their own organisations will be used to bring pressure on the party or the union. Thus it is to organisations like the Indian Workers' Associations that the individual looks to support him – a very practical kind of organisation which complements the more idealistic adherence to culture and religion.

There will, however, increasingly be a departure from this pattern. Some Indian children do not succeed at school or, even if they do, come to reject the Indian strategy of maintaining a separate society within, or alongside of, British society. Such young people have, to some extent, come to see the best hope as lying in joining with and encouraging white youth to join in the fight against all forms of inequality including racism. Such overtly political activity is becoming increasingly apparent amongst the Indian youth of Southall. For the moment, this means a *de facto* alliance with the far left, but it may well be that as Indians begin to influence local Labour parties they will not allow themselves to be isolated in this way.

Nearly all that we have said so far assumes that the Indian youth whom we are discussing are sane, balanced and rational individuals and it is, of course, right that we should do so because many of the manifestations of Indian behaviour which we have been discussing are sane, balanced, rational and sociologically understandable. But, if what Parsons teaches us about the socialisation process is true, we must surely assume that the immigration process will have broken families and destroyed the possibility of peaceful socialisation either in infancy or in adolescence. This is unknown territory for British social scientists. It could be, of course, that the extended kinship system provides a secure base for socialisation through parent substitutes and that the community is simply strengthened by the unity which it achieves in reaction to a racist immigration policy, but even then a people would have to be superhuman, or subhuman, for their children not to be affected and damaged by the family disruption caused by immigration and immigration control.

One final point to be made is this. Although Indians' children have, on the whole, performed surprisingly well at school, they have had to do so despite tremendous handicaps. If they lacked adequate English on arrival they might well have gone to areas where there was no language instruction available at all; they might well have gone to a language centre which provided no more than minimal English or, having taken English in withdrawal classes, may well have suffered because no thought had been given to the problem of their reinsertion into ordinary classes. It is not surprising, therefore, that amongst those who achieved only minimal exam passes while at school, there is now a not inconsiderable group of young men and women seeking to remedy their inadequate school education by adult education with a view to passing examinations. This group may well come to play an important part in community leadership in the future.

The structural and cultural situation of the West Indian immigrant is very different from that of the Asian minorities, and his children consequently face different problems. The key to the understanding of these differences lies in the heritage of slavery. Whereas the Asian minorities come from a complex empire within a larger empire and a long-term diaspora within that empire, the West Indians are drawn from a deliberately created colonial society in which the core institution was the slave plantation. Amongst the Asians there are wide-ranging class differences, educational differences and degrees of assimilation to British culture. Amongst West Indian migrants (to Britain at least) there is considerable uniformity of educational experience and class position; and there is the terrible fact that these people have been deprived of their ancestral culture and forced to live and to think in the cultural idiom and language of their masters.

One hears a great deal about the homeless, unemployed West Indian youth often affecting a Rastafarian lifestyle, and there is no doubt that such youths are crucial to the understanding of the cultural situation of black minorities in Britain. None the less it is important to recognise that this is not the lifestyle, as yet at least, of the majority. The West Indian majority are 'respectable' working-class people, many of whom go to church and are strongly oriented to British cultural values.

There is a remarkable difference between West Indian migration to Britain and to Canada. In Canada, West Indians are widely dispersed in white-collar work and banks, for example, are largely staffed in the clerical grades by West Indians and Chinese (from Hong Kong and Taiwan). Migrants to Britain are skilled, semi-skilled and unskilled workmen and if they do become socially mobile are liable to migrate back across the Atlantic to Canada. The result is an enormous degree of working-class uniformity. If it may be asked whether the Asian minorities in Britain face a Jewish future, it may equally be asked whether West Indians face an Irish future, that is whether, in the vast majority, they will enter the mainstream working class.

West Indian unemployment went down continuously from the moment of immigration so long as there was something like full employment (D. Smith, 1977). With the rise of unemployment, West Indian (and Asian) unemployment has increased disproportionately, but this does mean that there are a great many West Indian workers who have been continuously employed in the same job for five years or more. They filled gaps in the labour market and had little difficulty in establishing themselves as a permanent part of the labour force. What is striking in the sphere of unemployment, however, is that their children are far less welcome as workers, even though they may have qualifications superior to those of their parents.

Before we turn to their children, however, it is important that we should say something about the culture and society of the parents. There is nothing quite akin to the sharply differentiated culture and religion of the Asian minorities, but religion, at least, organises the community and shapes the thinking of the minority. No understanding of the West Indian immigrant or his children is possible, therefore, which omits reference to the churches.

Again, disappointing though it may be to those who live in expectation of the exotic, probably a majority of the church-going West Indians claim to be Anglican or Methodist. It is true, however, that orthodox Anglicanism or Methodism do not meet the cultural, social and spiritual needs of the community and that the Pentecostalist and Holiness churches command a commitment and a loyalty far greater amongst their members and they may well have greater long-term influence.

To go to a meeting of West Indian pastors from the Independent Churches is to enter a world of working-class religion which has largely disappeared amongst the native working class. There is a simple atmosphere of faith, a joy in communion and community, an unaffected enjoyment of singing and worship and a belief, above all, in the spontaneous and immediate action of the Holy Spirit rather than in a sacramental grace dispensed solely by ordained priests.

There is, of course, an element of ecstasy in this culture. To discover the fellowship of a West Indian congregation is to discover a kind of release and happiness which the mundane world of work does not allow. Yet, at the same time, there is a kind of puritanism and sobriety in contact with the world, which suggests that other forms of ecstasy are taboo. The church has no place for drink, and holds up its hands in holy horror at the behaviour of some West Indian youth. It seeks to make its own children respectable and disciplined and to a large extent it succeeds.

Such 'old-time religion', of course, presupposes its opposite and that opposite is to be found in the world of the marginalised individuals who are forced into unemployment or deliberately choose not to be proletarianised or, as Pryce has put it, to accept 'shit-work' (1979). There are other ways of living apart from being respectable workmen in an industrial society and a small minority of West Indians have chosen this way. They live with an eye on the main chance and, not being bound by the constraints which the Pentecostalist 'saints' impose on themselves, they find that the main chances which come their way carry a load of erotic satisfactions. They live by pimping, by cheating and thieving, and by peddling 'ganga' (marijuana) and some few live well in this way.

This deviant world is, of course, one which has links with popular music. Or perhaps better we should say that the world of popular music, which inevitably lives through its libidinal appeal, must take account of the world of the hustler amongst other worlds. Popular music in fact is one of the means whereby those who normally live in a world more cribbed and confined can yet gain some of the libidinal satisfaction which characterises the hustler's life.

There is, however, an alternative theme to those offered by the saints and the hustlers which is equally characteristic of West Indian life and which may, in the long run, be more important than either of them. This is the theme which goes back to the beginning of the West Indian's oppression and his cultural dilemma. It is the theme which says, 'We have been four hundred years in slavery. So-called emancipation did not fully right the wrong which had been done to us and it is that fundamental righting of the wrong which should now be the task of our people.'

The religious form of this doctrine is to be found in the teachings of the Rastafarian religion. We have seen above how the Pentecostal churches, with their emphasis upon the Holy Spirit rather than the apostolic succession as their means of communion with God, are already denying the religion and the ideology and the culture of the Establishment, but Pentecostalism none the less still tends towards quietism. A more fundamental challenge to secular as well as religious authority is therefore possible. Rastafarianism holds that the one black man who succeeded until the twentieth century in resisting colonialism, Haile Selassie, must have been divine and it is this religious doctrine which inserts itself into the religious scene and offers a religion which is not merely old-time but black.

But Rastafarianism, which derived from the teachings of the most influential of black political teachers, also has its secular counterpart. This is to be found in the political organisations of West Indians in Britain. From one point of view these have been disastrously ineffective. They have not, like the Indian Workers' Association and related Asian organisations, found ways of bringing pressure to bear on the British political system. What they have done, however, is to diagnose in non-obfuscating secular terms the wrong which is to be righted and, if they have not yet developed strategies for righting it, they have begun to mobilise the community in terms of secular revolutionary or secessionist beliefs.

To say that an individual is a West Indian child, then, is to be insufficiently specific. It is not simply that he will have come from one of a number of different islands or continental colonies hundreds of miles apart. That is something of less importance. The fact of the matter is that whether he is Jamaican, Barbadian, Kittician or Guyanese, he may come from a variety of different home-culture backgrounds, differentiated in terms of their degrees of conformity or deviance, their religious or secular nature, the degree to which they are rooted in discipline or ecstasy.

Perhaps the first thing to be noted is that in educational terms a small number of West Indian boys and girls do make it through the system. Geoffrey Driver has caused something of a sensation by pointing out that they who do so actually do better at school than their English counterparts (1980). Whatever doubts we may have about this, however, it is clear that, whereas amongst the immigrant parents' generation, few have stayed on at school after 15 and few have any qualifications, amongst those partially educated in Britain there is a tendency to stay on longer and gain qualifications, and amongst those wholly educated in Britain this tendency increases.

But getting O-levels of CSEs is not the whole story of education and socialisation in Britain. We have seen that in the anti-academic culture of the working classes in school, there is an alternative pattern of entry into the society via the life and the organisations of the working class. It is socialisation into this culture which is the achievement of many West Indian working-class boys and girls. One now meets young blacks along with white skinheads demonstrating in support of Tottenham Hotspur and, on a more acceptable level, one finds black youths taking their place amongst professional footballers and athletes as well as stars in black and racially mixed popular music groups (such involvements are the subject of Cashmore's work *Black Sportsmen*, 1982). It still remains to be seen whether acceptance into working-class youth society and its culture will be followed in the long run by entry into the life of the adult working class. So far we have seen evidence of black participation in strikes by the lower paid. The key problem here, however, is actual entry to employment. It may well be that being a part of working-class youth and its activities in and out of school does not involve equal participation in the employment market.

Working-class youth culture is, of course, a very varied entity. Differences in the class position of different groups, as well as changes in fashion and strategies for dealing with authority, have produced 'Teds,' 'rockers,' 'mods,' 'skinheads' – to name but a few of the styles of the last twenty years. It would be interesting to explore how far black affiliation to working-class youth involves affiliation to any of these. Oddly, there do seem to be possibilities of affiliation of young blacks even to those styles which have racist and fascist overtones. Blacks have, though rarely, participated in 'Paki-bashing'. What is more important, however, is that youth cultural style which is definitively black and asserts itself against all white groups, youth and culture alike. This is what is loosely called 'Rasta'. (For a fuller discussion of this, see the following chapter and especially Cashmore, 1979a.)

The selective systems which operate within schools, and in comprehensive schools no less than any other, appear to operate systematically against blacks. There are, of course, attempts to explain such selection as due to the hereditary qualities of the blacks as well as explanations which, while accepting that the rejected blacks do perform inadequately, blames that failure on the inadequacy of school resources (compare Eysenck, 1971, with Little, 1975). If, however, we are concerned with the process of socialisation and acculturation, other factors must come up for consideration. The fact is that in using English culture at all, let alone in trying to do well in it, the West Indian child faces unique difficulties. He has no other culture to turn to at home, as does, say, the Punjabi-speaking Sikh child, and the culture of his home and school alike are cultures which implicitly and explicitly devalue black people and their achievements. Starting with a low self-image he faces selective processes which present him with a further sense of his inadequacy. Such tests are difficult enough emotionally for the working-class English child to withstand. They are doubly difficult for the West Indian child, except in so far as his parents encourage him to show his superiority over his white working-class peers (Bagley and Verma, 1979).

All too often the West Indian child ends up in remedial or disciplinary class situations and once he is there the process becomes cumulative because teachers' stereotypes of West Indian children, formed in relation to what they see, become the basis for further processes of selection. For many West Indian children, therefore, it appears that the system is loaded against them and they take refuge in a culture which urges them to take pride in their own black culture, while treating school as time to be filled in, as a trial which one has to bear. Rasta, amongst other things, helps to restore the self-esteem of the remedials and the low streamers, just as working-class youth culture offers self-justification to the 'non-academic' 60 per cent.

This is not, however, the whole story. Rejection in the selective process in schools is only one of three breaches with society that the West Indian child experiences. The others may be with his family and with the world of work. Unlike the Asian family which makes a break between even young adults and their parents virtually impossible, the link between a young West Indian male and his parents is relatively weak. Although the matricentral family thesis (discussed by Clarke, 1966) has decreasing relevance to British experience (see Rex and Tomlinson, 1979, ch. 3), it is still the case that young males may not be expected to live at home after they have left school and many West Indian boys do, in fact, move out. They are even more likely to do so if there is a gap between their parents' desire for conformity and achievement and their own experience of its impossibility. It would be interesting to compare the achievements of children of religious and non-religious parents in this respect.

Whether or not young blacks succeed educationally, they are likely to suffer a similar experience of rejection when they seek employment. Discrimination against young working-class blacks is widespread at all levels of employment. This is a situation which requires diagnosis and rationalisation. One option is by opting out of the world of employment altogether and affiliating to the marginal culture of the hustlers. The other is to turn to the sort of political and religious diagnosis of Rastafari.

Young men (and women) do not normally turn to religious movements for explanations of their rejection and their deviance. If they are to be affected by ideas such as those Rastafarianism has to offer there must be some intervening medium through which ideas are conveyed to them. That medium is provided by reggae music. Along with the more libidinal ecstatic messages which they receive from its beats and its themes, they also receive a political message which speaks to their condition (see Troyna, 1977*a*). The one word 'Babylon' repeated again and again in their lyrics conveys to them the whole message of 'four hundred years of slavery', as well as of the injustices to which the selective system has subjected them. It seems to perform exactly the function which the slogan 'Black Power' performed for young American blacks in the 1960s. (The importance of 'Babylon' to black youth generally is underlined in Chapter 2.)

The culture of popular black music, which we suggested earlier drew on the 'illegitimate' feelings of the hustler culture, is in fact a very complex phenomenon indeed. It does have a sheerly libidinal element, but it also reproduces some of the religious ecstasy of the sects. Hence one should not be surprised to hear irreligious young blacks singing and dancing to songs about being born again. But religious, political and libidinal elements are combined when reference is made to Babylon, captivity and the possibility of escape and return to the Black Jerusalem.

It is commonly suggested that the young men who become 'Rasta' are really only a sham version of the real thing. They are called 'fashion-dreads' (who wear 'dreadlocks' as a matter of fashion rather than out of religious commitment) or are accused of accepting 'half-digested gobbets' of Rasta teaching (J. Brown, 1977). The actual life and practice of the young Rastas, however, is more complex than this. Young Rastas may live in squats and smoke ganga, but they also read the Bible which, to say the least of it, is a rare-enough activity amongst young delinquents. The fact is that the Rasta lifestyle has its own meanings and its own religious significance equivalent to that of either the mainstream Rastafarian Church or the Pentecostal and Holiness Churches. But, whereas they may be brought into relation to mainstream life by co-option to the Council of Churches or the Ministers Fraternal, the Rastas of the streets remain stubbornly unclubbable.

Young Rastafarians gather on street corners. Young thieves gather on street corners. Some marginalised men gather on street corners. Some Rastas are thieves and marginalised men. Some marginalised men become thieves and Rastas, or both. Some young Rastas are simply lawfully and peacefully going about their business. But the police, in the task of preventing crime (in the literal sense of pre-venting), stop, question and harass the most visible of those on the street corners – the Rastas. The police station itself comes to be called Babylon and the whole recurrent theme of the captivity is enacted and dramatised once again.

We began the part of this chapter which discusses young West Indians by saying that the young homeless, unemployed Rasta was not the typical West Indian youth. But, as we have talked about all the other cultural possibilities open to West Indians, it has become obvious that the drama of Rasta is meaningful to all of them. The Pentecostalist knows what is meant by Babylon even if his notion of being born again is more spiritual than that of the Rastas. The hustler joins him in his use of ganga as well as other aspects of his deviance, and all are aware in some measure of police repression as a ubiquitous element of black life. The alternatives to Rasta are really only two – successful entry into the working class or successful passage through the working class in the culture of the schools.

The presentation of this chapter, some may justifiably claim, has been sexist. We have talked about boys or, where we have spoken about boys and girls collectively, we have used the term 'he' or 'him'. This is because the neutral pronoun 'her' has not yet gained universal acceptance. There are, however, many problems to be explored about the different fates of Asian and West Indian girls as well as boys.

Both the groups or cultures which we have been discussing are themselves 'sexist', the Asian culture in a deep patriarchal sense and the West Indian in the sense that males do have greater freedom from domestic and parental obligations than females. To understand the situations of Asian and West Indian girls, therefore, we should have to explore the ways in which they confront not merely the problems of their encounter with British culture but also the attempts which they make to protect themselves against, or resist, male dominance.

This is one of the themes of Chapter 6. It is, however, worth pointing out one or two differences between the situation *vis-à-vis* their menfolk of the two groups of girls. Asian girls do not merely participate in a division of labour with their fathers and husbands. They are also controlled by them and some find that control oppressive, particularly when new models are made apparent to them by the cultures to which they are exposed – even though they have reason to oppose these other cultures because of the injustices perpetrated in their name. By contrast, the West Indian female has a great degree of freedom. Far from being oppressed by her menfolk she may taunt them and even bully them. But it is the ultimate fact of maternity which defines her condition. In bringing up her children she will be cut off from the normal labour market and forced to do inferior part-time work while her man lives about the town to an extent unknown amongst Asian patriarchs.

In these last comments on girls and women we may be accused of dealing in generalisations and stereotypes. The same charge may be levelled against the chapter as a whole. This is to be accepted. The chapter, however, is as an attempt to indicate the nature of a typology of youth situations – class youth situations and minority youth situations. The research to which it points is not towards simple cross-tabulations of life-chances and social conditions so dearly loved by British empirical sociology, but to the collection of structured life histories to see how far these ideal types or stereotypes actually reflect the range of empirical reality. An essay such as this is only a first step towards research and understanding. But without such a first step, research into, and understanding of, the problems of youth are hardly possible.

5 Growing Up in Babylon

ERNEST CASHMORE and BARRY TROYNA

Introduction: 'Look to Africa ...'

Before the 1970s, few people in England had heard of the movement called Ras Tafari. Those who were familiar with it were, in the main, Jamaican migrants who had experienced first-hand contact with it in their native land where the movement arose in the early 1930s. The preceding period had seen the spectacular rise and ignominious demise of Marcus Garvey, the founder and leader of the Universal Negro Improvement Association which sought to return all black peoples to their 'fatherland', Africa. Though failing in his stated aims of mass migration, the Jamaican-born leader mobilised sentiment of such intensity that his influence was to linger on for generations. Indeed, Garvey himself anticipated the longevity of his vision: 'Be assured I planted well the seed of Negro or black nationalism' (1967, Vol. 2, p. 237).

What Garvey actually did, however, is less important than the mythology which developed around him. He became elevated to the role of prophet by early Rastafarian leaders who saw him as the harbinger of a new age. The disparity between the man and the myth surrounding him was bridged by the attribution of a single undocumented phrase: 'Look to Africa when a black king shall be crowned, for the day of deliverance is near.' Around this, a total belief system and, indeed, a new conception of reality was created.

In 1930 events in Ethiopia seemed to portend the salvation of black peoples; in November of that year Prince Ras Tafari was crowned Emperor of Ethiopia and invested with his official title, Haile Selassie I, King of Kings, Lord of Lords, the all-conquering Lion of the Tribe of Judah. When the event was reported in the Jamaican press, Garvey's more enthusiastic supporters made the link between their leader's black king and the new emperor. Ras Tafari was to be the redeemer of all blacks and it was he who would arrange for them to be transported to Africa. His ability to do this was founded on the simple premiss that he was God or, in Rastafarian terms, Jah (see Revelation 5:2–5 and 19:16).

At no time did Garvey publicly acknowledge the legitimacy of the Rastafarian enterprise nor the divinity of the emperor. Indeed, ironically, Garvey denounced Haile Selassie as 'a great coward' and of 'playing white' after the Italian conquest of Ethiopia in 1935. Garvey also castigated the emperor for being the ruler of a country where black men are chained and flogged' (quoted in Cronon, 1974, p. 162). The myth, on the other hand, became immeasurably bigger than the man and thousands of black Jamaicans prepared energetically for the supernaturally wrought transportation which would precede the dissolution of the white man's domination, characterised by the Rastas as 'Babylon'. (For more detail on the Jamaican movement see Simpson, 1955a, 1955b, 1962; Smith, Augier and Nettleford, 1967; Barrett, 1977.)

Needless to say, the miraculous African redemption did not materialise and the structure of Babylon remained intact. But so, too, did the commitment in the inevitability of a worldly transformation and, by the late 1970s, the vision of a redeemed Africa had spread to the urban areas of Britain, seizing the hearts and imaginations of tens of thousands of black youths and impelling them to new modes of thought and postures of defiance (see Cashmore, 1977, 1979a, 1979b). The growing awareness that Haile Selassie was the true God and the concomitant realisation that conventional Christianity was a masquerade perpetrated by the white man to expedite his total domination, both physically and mentally, bred new feelings of resentment and antagonism amongst a sizeable number of black youths. As the 1970s progressed, more and more young blacks immersed themselves in the movement and simultaneously broadened the virtually unbridgeable chasm between the first- and second-generation migrants.

The original migrants from the West Indies had experienced the fractures of migration and the sharp prongs of racialism in the 1950s and 1960s but had articulated the desire to improve conditions through involvement with localised churches (see Calley, 1965; Hill, 1971). But their children became drawn by the vision of a Messianic consummation of history and this was to have profound behavioural consequences. The cultivation of their hair into long and unkempt 'dreadlocks' and the adoption of the Ethiopian national colours of red, green and black, signified the black youths' outright rejection of society and their allegiance to Africa (used synonomously with Ethiopia); their nurturance of a stylised Jamaican patois, a language of fictive kinship, exteriorised the essential brotherhood of all blacks; and their refusal to co-operate at any level with agencies of what they called 'the race-relations industry' or anything tainted with the influence of Babylon demonstrated their intention to detach themselves from the wider society and crystallise into their own communities.

The movement of Ras Tafari constituted a complete rupture with the first generation and, in many ways, characterised the qualitatively different life experiences of the two groups. What, on the surface, might have seemed bizarre indulgence or escapist fantasy was, on analysis, a revealing glimpse at the contrasting orientations of first- and second-generation West Indians. The movement towards the open defiance and rejection of society suggests massive changes in consciousness; such changes are the focus for this chapter.

Affiliation to the Rastafarian movement involved two sets of conditions: the commissioning ones being the availability of Rastafarian concepts and themes and the vehicles for their transmission; the facilitating ones being the existence of high degrees of suggestibility among the black community in England. Much has been written about the growth in popularity of Jamaican reggae music, complete with Rastafarian afflatus (Kallynder and Dalrymple, 1974; Troyna, 1978c) and the formation of the black gang structures which acted as channels for the communication of Rastafarian themes (Troyna, 1978a). What remains unclear, however, is how the youths became progressively involved in the movement, adopting its symbols, motifs and emblems and immersing themselves in the belief system to the point where they accepted the divinity of Jah Ras Tafari and, by implication, the inevitability of a 'return' to Africa.

The process of becoming a Rastaman can be divided into four broad phases: first, the apprehension of racial disadvantage; secondly, the loss of plausibility of parents' beliefs; thirdly, the drift to Ras Tafari; and fourthly, the acceptance of Haile Selassie. This affiliation to the Rastas should be regarded as a complex and not always unhindered transfer of allegiances involving the transgression of certain rules and principles peculiar to West Indian life in Britain, and the crossing of psychological bridges leading to the new reality. As such, the process of affiliation is fraught with obstacles in the form of familial pressures, public stigmatisation, countervailing definitions of reality and denials of legitimacy. Yet, despite these roadblocks, there was a growth in the number of black youths who were able to carry through this 'Journey'. In order to do this, the potential Rastaman had to undergo a series of cognitive rearrangements which were triggered off by experiences and apprehensions of a very specific nature. Our reasons for suggesting this arise from our reflections on two independent pieces of research on black youth in Britain in the late 1970s. (See Troyna, 1978*b*; Cashmore, 1979*a*. Unless otherwise stated, the conversational extracts in this chapter are taken from those studies.)

The Apprehension

> My close friends are West Indian – I can trust them, whites are too greedy. But Chris is a good friend 'cos he knows a lot of things about coloured people. He wears the clothes like the coloureds and he likes reggae. The only thing wrong with him is that he's just white. (A 15-year-old student at a North London secondary school)

It would obviously be futile to deny the importance of the immediate post-school years in the youth's travel along the road to Jah. It is during these years, when the black school-leaver first enters into competition with his white counterparts for a job, that the iniquities of racialism in Britain make their most profound impact. There is now ample documentation, both at local and national levels, showing the disproportionately high level of unemployment amongst youths of West Indian origin, a trend which cannot be accounted for simply by differences in educational achievement. A recent survey of black and white school-leavers in Lewisham, for instance, pointed out that 'at many levels of educational achievement blacks were more likely to be unemployed than whites' (CRE, 1978*a*; see also Boyd, 1978; CRE, 1980*b*).

Nevertheless, Ken Pryce is clearly overstating the point when he characterises the immediate post-school years as ones in which 'the process of alienation *begins* for the West Indian' (Pryce, 1979, p. 125, emphasis added). On the contrary, it is possible to trace the formative stages of this process back to the later stages of the youths' secondary-school education. It is during these years that they begin to realise that their skin colour is disparaged in the wider society and that it can be, and often is, used as a basis for exclusion and rejection; as one Rasta reflected: 'When did I realise racialism existed? Just before I left school, I guess. When it seemed people treated me differently because I was black and for no other reason. Before that I didn't give the matter too much thought.'

One of our studies of black youth cultures in secondary schools in London and the East Midlands both substantiates and confirms the importance of these years in the progressive estrangement of these young blacks from the mainstream of society. The youths were all in their final year at school and were already sensitive to the limits which racial discrimination was to impose on their life-chances. For example, many of them mentioned older friends and relatives who had failed to get a job because of alleged discrimination:

> I think lots of them haven't got jobs because they're coloured. Lots of coloured people haven't got jobs. When I come home from school, there's all coloured boys in the park lying down.

While others were reconciled to facing similar problems in their own search for work:

> Some of them [employers] are prejudiced. That worries me 'cos when I go to get a job and I've got the right certificates for it, because I'm not the same colour I'm cheated out of a job. I don't like that 'cos I've been cheated.

The youths' own experiences of racism and discrimination centred around confrontations with the police both locally and, for the youths in London in particular, at the annual Notting Hill Carnival. They gave plenty of examples of how the police harassed them, simply because of their skin colour and how, for the same reason, they had been victims of police brutality. To take one:

> We had a fight with the police in Wood Green. We smashed their walkie-talkies. Had to go to court. They were telling lies in court. They pick on you because you're coloured. When we were going into the van they were pushing us and calling us black bastards.

And another:

> They pull you in and give you a big belting. It's happened to me twice. They beat me up, kicking me in the belly and in the back.

Importantly, many of the youths explained police attitudes and behaviour towards blacks in terms of general attitudes and behaviour towards black people in Britain. Why, they asked, should these be any different? After all, 'it's only the uniform which tells them apart.'

Their apprehension of racial disadvantage both directly, through their experiences with the police, and indirectly, through hearing of the frustrations in the search for work, sparked off a pattern of events which was to foster the formation of a distinctly British Rastafarian movement. Unlike their parents, who had obviously gained an awareness of British racism and racialism through their involvement in both labour and housing markets (Daniel, 1968; Carby and Thakur, 1977; D. Smith, 1977; and Burney, 1967; Rex and Moore, 1967) these youths were unable to hark back and compare current circumstances with those of 'home'. Such buffering factors were simply not available to these young blacks, most of whom had been born, or at least had spent most of their life, in this country. So, as one youth expressed it: 'It's no good wanting to go back there to the West Indies. You've got to stand up and fight here.'

When the realisation was reached that both they and their parents had been, and would continue to be, denied entry into positions of authority and prestige, choice accommodation and certain services because of skin colour, they had few resources with which to minimise the severity of the shock, assuage the anxieties, or even rationalise their disappointment. The awareness that their progress would be (and possibly had already been) retarded by their blackness fused that blackness with a fresh symbolic meaning and social arrangements came to be organised around that meaning. It became the basis for the orientation of activities both in and out of school and the result was the crystallisation of young blacks, particularly those in the lower academic streams, into gangs. One black pupil reckoned: 'When you're small it doesn't matter, but as you grow up you don't push yourself away, but it's like something in the middle pushing you away', while another insisted: 'I don't think any of my friends are proper, proper English. I don't like the way they go with their dirty jeans and their long, long hair. I don't like their culture.'

This withdrawal into exclusively black gangs resulted from a common awareness of situation and a conviction that the situation is unalterably affected by their being black. As one Rastaman was to express it: 'It is inevitable that we, as black people, were never and can never be part of this country where we do not belong; like a heart transplant, it rejects us.'

The Loss

The emergence of a gang structure and the perception of blackness as an impediment to progress and integration together worked to weaken the young blacks' ties with the parental culture. As we have already shown, links were loosened by the first dawn of realisation of racialism in the later stages of secondary education and, as the structure of the gangs was consolidated, the important socialising functions of the family passed over to the peer group. This unit assumed primacy as the vehicle for transmitting thoughts and values. One youth spoke for his friends: 'We always talk about music, it helps us to learn things. You get records telling you a story, telling you the facts.

Like the Rasta records, that's learning and we talk about it.' Now, familial fragmentation after migration, inadequate housing, employment that required sometimes both parents working long and awkward hours placed pressures on the family's role in socialisation. But this was further exacerbated by the ability of the youth to be cognisant of his parents' position in relation to his own and their common characteristic of blackness. In a Rasta's own words, the parents were '*fooling themselves*; they're never going to be accepted as equals in this society'.

The apprehension that their parents were somehow engaged in a self-defeating endeavour introduced all manner of complications into the parent–child relationship and an earnest questioning, if not criticism, of parental postures and beliefs led to the association of attitudes and religion. As Berger (1969, p. 42) would express it, the 'plausibility structure' of the parents' beliefs lost firmness. But the mere loosening of allegiances to the first generation's religions did not necessarily imply an outright rejection of them; they were the unfocused murmurs of discontent and unease rather than wholesale condemnations. And here lies the importance of Rastafarian-inspired reggae music in supplying black youths with the theoretical equipment with which to make sense out of their parents' positions, their beliefs and their ambitions. Armed with the Rastafarian world-view, the young blacks were able to slot everything into place and the first generation's lack of anything resembling assertion of presence, let alone defiance, became more understandable:

> Our parents, you know, they have all been so brainwashed – well, some of them anyway.
>   How could our parents give I and I anything to live up to? They've been misguided by European Christianity which is not acceptable to Rasta and so are still suffering the effects in their bodies and their minds.

Increasing familiarity with Rastafarian themes and concepts provided the suggestible black youth, alarmed by the existence of racialism and uncommitted in his affiliation to parental world-views, with the means for understanding the mechanism through which the white man's Babylon retained its grip on the world and, in so doing, suppressed the potentialities of the black population; what Rastas would call the denial of the 'true self'.

> After seeing the true self, other religions were without significance to I and I ... Pentecostal and Methodist and various other churches; you know, we didn't accept that because they derived from the European. We know that in ourself we had to do something black because we are black.

Critical examination of the structures and mechanisms which underpinned white control, both physical and mental, over the black man produced a new apprehension of the world and an appreciation of the role of the black man come the transformation of that world. But the examination could not have taken place on the scale it did without the structure of gangs. Had it not been for the existence of an established gang structure, the Rastafarian themes filtering across via reggae music would have had no vehicle for their transmission.

The Drift

The process of the transmission was called 'reasoning', informal but regular intra-gang and inter-gang interaction. Groups would come together quite spontaneously to engage in often protracted dialogues concerning a limitless range of topics. Foci for the discussion would vacillate between the profound, perhaps a matter of Scriptural interpretation, to the unexceptional, possibly the merits of a piece of music. The undulating dialogue might change topic in a rather flightly fashion and participants would come and go without interrupting the flow of conversation. Central to the reasoning was the Rastafarian grid through which all dialogue was to be filtered. All subjects were to be made sense of in terms of a specific interpretive matrix, the skeleton of which was supplied by the inspirational messages of Big Youth, U. Roy, Burning Spear, Fred Locks and, of course, the archetypal Rastaman, Bob Marley.

The reggae music of the 1970s fell upon receptive and suggestible ears but there was no direct imprint on to a passive black community; rather a process of cumulative interpretation whereby the black youth to whom the parental culture had lost credibility seized upon the basic Rastafarian themes of reggae and attempted to anchor them in his personal experience. A youth reflected on his initial contact with Rasta ideas:

> First time was reading through *Rastaman Vibrations* [a Bob Marley LP]; I always thought that he was chatting rubbish then I read the words – played back his other records and found that it wasn't rubbish he was chatting. It was about the Rastas.

It was from this important starting-point that the youth critically debated broad issues and discussed minutiae whilst all the time acquiring what he considered to be 'insight'. Asked about the relative importance of music, a Rastaman answered: 'Maybe music was the inspiration for the movement, but through reasoning a better understanding was reached.' It was an understanding which provided the youth with this important quality of insight, the ability to see and comprehend the world through a Rastafarian grid.

The acquisition of insight and the new cognitive and normative directives it implied was underpinned by what we characterise as a process of 'drift', a motion in which the youth became progressively attached to the movement. The drift was guided by two sets of influences: the facilitating ones being the loss of commitment to the parental culture; the promotional ones deriving from the availability of Rastafarian concepts and the social apparatus for their transmission.

So, then, the enduring structure of the black gang provided ready-made channels for the communication of Rastafarian ideas; the smooth transmission was lubricated by regular, stable patterns of social interaction among young blacks. Homogeneity, similarity of orientation and social condition ensured a more or less uniform reception for the messages of reggae. Familiarity with Ras Tafari was self-generating once the initial awareness had been approached by one or more gang members. Full comprehension of the doctrines and normative prescriptions was not necessary for the drifter because being a Rastaman was always 'a process of becoming'. As one of us was told on numerous occasions, 'the learning never stops'. Knowledge of the faith gained during the drift was always penumbral and to claim full insight was tantamount to a breach of faith. However, once the boundaries of Ras Tafari had been broached, then the drift towards the nucleus of beliefs and the cognitive and normative elements involved could begin.

The dislocation from the culture of the first generation became more complete as the drift towards Ras Tafari intensified and the youth acquired sufficient insight to comprehend his elders' dispositions: 'The majority of blacks in this country are still in a state of mind that can be described as not a conscious state of mind; they still believe they are perhaps inferior.' On the other hand, the youth had begun to rid himself of this self-image of inferiority and embarked on a voyage of self-discovery. One young black proclaimed that:

Reggae has helped me with history anyway. If it wasn't for these kinds of records black people would be in the dark about what did happen in Africa. Black people came from Africa but with the slave trade they took them from Africa and some stayed in Jamaica and some stayed in England.

The Rasta wanted to eulogise his African ancestry and revive the 'true self': 'It's for I and I to revive our true self and really know our ability by discovering our history and by discovering our history we know what we were capable of in thé past.' The drift entailed reversing the postures of the first generation which the Rastas considered had internalised whites' definitions of the negro as inferior and promoting the 'true self', the black man who had realised his African roots through successive acquisitions of insight. One implication of this was that the Rastaman, in total contrast to the majority of blacks, was in the company of an élite minority, a chosen few who had developed a greater understanding of the world and were privy to at least some of the secrets which enabled the white man to subordinate the black. An important consequence of this was that the company of the discredited agents of Babylon, or those unable to penetrate its mystique, was devalued; contacts were restricted to those enlightened ones who were prepared to abandon their involvement with the wider society and engage in the search for the true self. Relationships with outsiders were systematically broken as the drifting continued and the processes of inclusion (of insiders) and exclusion (of outsiders) worked to seal the Rastas into practically impermeable spheres.

Closing the ranks to non-Rastas brought forward sometimes punitive responses from outsiders and this, in turn, consolidated the feeling of exclusivity and élitism, 'they [other blacks] see that Rastafarian make it bad for your own group, you know, and in a way they don't believe in themself as black people'. Breakdowns in relationships with those outside the movement were of little consequence to the drifter for he envisioned himself as an enlightened person, a man of insight who had little to gain from contact with those tainted by the noxious influence of Babylon. As the drift progressed, it became clear that the uncomprehending wider society would always reject the validity of Rastafarian beliefs: 'them never understand I and I; so I don't need them'. The movement was all the member needed; it gave him the support and confidence and strengthened the plausibility structure of Ras Tafari to the extent where the youth came to accept the divinity of Haile Selassie: 'I used to reason with my brothers here; and, you know, I gradually get the insight, begin to see clearer the truth; yes, I come to accept His Imperial Majesty Selassie I as God Almighty.'

The Acceptance

Strictly speaking, the acceptance of Haile Selassie as the divine redeemer of black people, and the concomitant belief in his ability and intention to instigate a transformation of the social cosmos in which Babylon would be destroyed and blacks returned to Africa, were never regarded as a conscious, deliberate decision by the Rastaman himself. As far as the individual was concerned, he was always a Rasta, it just being a matter of time before he realised this. 'Jah passed over I' and 'It was in us from creation' were typical responses to the question of how they came to such a realisation: 'One day I came to accept His Imperial Majesty as the true Lord.' Accepting Haile Selassie was no snap decision, but a culmination of the acquisition and internalisation of Rastafarian ideas, themes and categories, insight, in which the youth's awareness broadened with each successive reasoning session. As a Rastaman expressed it: 'Man learns through reasoning; this is how the brethren reaches enlightenment and comes to understand his true self.' And 'understanding the true self' was vitally important to the acceptance, for they were to be regarded as two aspects of the same phenomenon. Accepting Haile Selassie as God entailed acknowledging that he was also inhering in all Rastas. It was central to Rastafarian belief that Jah was not only above men but in all men, a belief expressed in the principle of 'I and I': 'I and I means that God is in all men. The bond of Ras Tafari is the bond of God, of man. But man itself needs a head and the head of man is His Imperial Majesty Haile Selassie of Ethiopia.'

It becomes apparent that the unifying bond which linked the Rastas together was this belief in a brotherhood. Entry into the Rastafarian movement meant being cognisant of a fraternity of brethren united by the presence of Ras Tafari in all members. The awareness brought with it a fresh feeling of belongingness, of unity with fellow-members. A Rastaman explained: 'I-man him not individualistic or any stuff like that; he has his brethren ... these are my brethren; I am to them as they are to I.' And another: 'When he's [a Rastaman] addressing a brethren as himself, he says I and I – as being the oneness of two persons. So, God is within all of us and *we're all one people*.' The notion of being 'all one people' was immensely important in promoting the in-group solidarity and feeling of we-ness that characterised the movement. Accepting Haile Selassie involved no elaborate rituals or oath-taking; it was a simple self-realisation, a recognition that God was within oneself. But it was a recognition which brought with it admission to a realm where all fellow Rastas coexisted in and for the movement and, therefore, each other. For the young black, dispirited at his perception of the restricted opportunities available to him and distraught at his lack of normative direction, the new membership of an all-pervasive brotherhood was a morally uplifting experience. The dissipation of energies which had occurred in previous years was seen as a fragment of the past: 'Since accepting Ras Tafari I am a reformed man. I used to be in trouble with the police and all that foolishness; but now I have insight enough to know I was foolish.'

Acceptance brought with it a retrospective interpretation of the world and the self; past events were re-read through a Rastafarian grid: 'Being a Rasta, I understand more clearly why I as a black person I was oppressed and made to suffer. Babylon, this beats down on I just 'cause I black. Just like it has done for four hundred years.' As well as understanding his parents' passivity and his own enervation before the drift to Ras Tafari, the youth was able to comprehend the entire history of black people in terms of an elaborate conspiracy designed and orchestrated by Babylon to suppress black people and prevent them from realising their true potential in all spheres – cultural, political, economic, and so on. Because of their lack of military resources and their predilection to pursue cultural achievements, Africans were open targets for the Europeans at the inception of slavery. Denial of freedom, cognitive and material, was a necessary condition for the perpetuation of slavery and every subsequent event in the development of black–white contact was to be understood as a recycling of this early pattern. A Rasta observed: 'I and I now understand how the Imperial Machine of the West and the religions that served it were designed to oppress all black peoples in the world.' But the Rastaman did not need to delve into history books for evidence of this; he found it in his everyday experience of 'suffering' which was both immediate and transhistorical: 'It's *all* about suffering: the black man has been trodden on for four hundred years and there's no reason why Babylon won't try to keep it that way.' Furthermore, acceptance of Haile Selassie and the wealth of insight this brought was thought to alert Babylon to the imminent threat of the enlightened Rastaman who could clearly see the machinery serving to enslave him: 'Babylon has seen the Rastaman and must tremble in his presence.' And so extra pressure would be brought to bear: 'now we must struggle even harder' but 'the faith is the strength to overcome the oppression'.

Acceptance made the world fully transparent to the Rastaman and equipped him with the knowledge of the deceptions at work to obfuscate the black man's vision and stifle his natural capacities. For this reason it was necessary to cast a critical eye on every event impinging on the experience of the black man. Obviously, the Bible was subject to exegetical scrutiny with the Rastaman trying to sift out the mistranslations, amendments and omissions which the whites had artfully and surreptitiously weaved into the Scriptures; but also newspaper and magazine articles, books and various government reports had to be regarded with caution. The source of any information contrary to Rastafarian expectation was to be established before any judgement on it could be made and, if the source was connected with Babylon, then the knowledge could be construed as self-serving ideology. As one Rastaman retorted when confronted with newspaper reports on the death of Haile Selassie in 1975: 'Imperial propaganda ... lies of the West.' Outside sources of information were endowed with a negative status and Rastafarian sources were validated with a strategy Berger and Luckmann (1972, p. 132) call 'nihilation': 'to liquidate conceptually everything *outside*'. Phenomena which did not square with the Rastafarian interpretation of the world were denied credibility and dismissed – except as further evidence of the conspiracy. Through nihilating outsiders' versions, the Rastaman insulated himself from potentially damaging phenomena and thus strengthened the subjective plausibility of Ras Tafari. All events in the world were to be comprehended in the context of the conspiracy; but it was a conspiracy with a time-limit.

The resolution to the black man's plight was simple but comprehensive: the dissolution of Babylon. Though the precise manner in which this was to come about was never spelt out with any clarity, the Rastaman, upon accepting Haile Selassie, became total in the conviction that the cosmic transformation was inevitable and that it was to be God's will. 'Must come' and 'this is the last days' were typical endorsements of the future cataclysm and the Book of Revelation was often cited as supportive of this: 'According to the prophecy of Revelation, the beast shall emerge in the last days. We now see the rise of the Common Market and we see that it is written in Revelations that my children are to leave Babylon.'

Acceptance, then, required the Rastaman to immerse himself into a fraternity of brethren by acknowledging the unity of all Rastas through the bond of God, to subscribe to an encyclopaedic theory which explained the development of black subordination and to become unshakeable in the conviction that the white man's grip was at an end.

Conclusion: The Journey Continues

The phenomenal growth of the Rastafarian movement during the late 1970s indicates that the acceptance of Haile Selassie became arguably the most important feature of the second-generation West Indian community. Quite literally, tens of thousands of young blacks embarked on their journeys to Jah, loosening their allegiances to their parents and the culture they represented and drifting towards the eventual acceptance of Haile Selassie. They became inspired by a vision of a transformed world in which all black peoples would be returned to their rightful homeland, Africa. But the vision itself was less important than the dispositions and postures it provoked. The Rastas became disenchanted with their parents, with whites and with society generally; they grew resentful of the racialism which they understood to be built into a structure designed to perpetuate the domination of Babylon. Membership of the movement prompted a new consciousness; the Rastaman considered himself to have acquired insight. What was, for the first generation, opaque was, for the Rasta, transparent. The methods and tactics employed by whites to maintain their control were no secret for him; they were apprehensible within the Rastafarian framework.

The whole Rastafarian enterprise had the effect of morally uplifting the young black and instilling in him a new morale and sense of selfhood, 'the true self' as opposed to that image offered by white society. A polarisation from the rest of society was inevitable. But it was the remoteness which gave the Rastaman the sense of belonging to an exclusive and, in many ways, élite movement. As far as he was concerned his reliance on the rest of society was over and he could simply wait for its destruction – and, conversely, his own deliverance.

Changes in the consciousness of these youths were dramatic and comprehensive. So complete was the reversal of postures that it was difficult to imagine that just one generation separated the Rastas from the original migrants. The Rastaman was suddenly purged of mendacious beliefs, liberated from old ways, given new commands and plunged into a struggle of almost apocalyptic proportions. His endeavour was to disengage his associations with the rest of society and retire into enclaves in expectation of the coming cataclysm and the perfect future it heralded.

It may be too early to assess the long-term impact of these changes. It would be facile to conclude that because Babylon will not fall and Rastas will not be returned to their perceived fatherland that the movement will fade into insignificance as fine dreams die and black youths work out alternative, and possibly more practicable, recipes for their futures. The subjective changes involved in the process of becoming a Rastaman were total and, in all probability, irrevocable. Once insight had been achieved it was unlikely that the Rasta would surrender his perspicacity for obscurity. In the mind of the Rastaman, only he and his fellow brethren had pierced the rhetoric of Babylon and fully understood their own positions *vis à vis* the rest of the world. The journey to Jah was accompanied by a solidifying of the subjective plausibility and a hardening of resolution to remain separate from anything attempting to undermine Rastafarian beliefs. We close with a Rastaman's articulation of this: 'I and I now see that Babylon has enslaved the black man even mentally. But the I man has the insight to see through this and he want no part of Babylon. *Time will show the truth of Ras Tafari.*'

6 Young, Female and Black

MARY FULLER

> ... women hold up far more than half the sky – but we are not about to make a religion out of womanhood as a state of grace or style of work: there's a world of difference between working harder and being more powerful ... (Wilmette Brown, 1980)

I want to do two things in this chapter. First I want to describe a group of black adolescent girls who were pupils in the London comprehensive school where I carried out research between 1975 and 1977, whilst employed at the Social Science Research Council Unit on Ethnic Relations, Bristol. These pupils formed a discernible subculture within the school. Its existence and specific defining features call into question some of our present assumptions about black pupils and about the nature of school-based subcultures. By concentrating on black adolescent girls I hope to make some contribution to altering the very strong emphasis on males and whites which is so striking in the literature documenting and analysing the experiential world of adolescents in and out of school. I also hope to show that treating black pupils as a sexually undifferentiated entity, as many writers continue to do (see, for example, Little, 1975), avoids confronting some important differences in the ways in which females and males may manifest resistance to racism in the school context.

My second and related aim is to locate the study of the subculture within a theoretical perspective which analyses rather than obscures female subordination. Three themes are important here. The empirical study illuminates the ways in which the double subordination of being black and female structures the consciousness of a specific group of adolescent girls in the particular context of a school. By concentrating on how the girls perceive themselves as black and female it is possible to look at the sometimes complex links between double subordination and the formation of consciousness. Finally, the finding from this study will be compared with the conclusions drawn from other recent work on black female pupils. This will show how, using some conceptual sleights of hand, it has been possible for other commentators to contribute to the myth that black women are not subordinated on the basis of their sex and, indeed, may even be 'privileged' in relation to other women.

Within the social formation blacks are subordinated through relations of racial domination and women are subordinated through relations of sexual domination. Domination is at the level of the material and ideological. Exclusion operates in the areas of law, housing, welfare, education and employment.

Schooling, together with the family and mass media, are seen as the institutions in which dominant ideologies are transmitted; that is, institutions predicated on dominant ideologies and through which both oppressors and oppressed learn those ideologies. What is missing from these formulations is some model of the ways in which material and ideological domination structures are incorporated into the consciousness of those who are subordinated. Fanon (1967) has written of the mechanisms and psychic consequences of such oppression for those who are racially oppressed, while Mitchell (1975) has discussed the similar effects for those who are oppressed because of their sex. In both instances, it is suggested, part of the oppression lies in being unable to see clearly that one *is* dominated – the values and attitudes of the dominant group are internalised and turned against the self; self-oppression becomes the means whereby resistance to the oppressor becomes literally almost unthinkable; self-hate, low self-esteem, fear of the oppressor are the outcomes. Powerful as such pressures are it is clear that the existence within a patriarchal and racist society of black and female resistance to racism and sexism in itself demonstrates that the development of consciousness is not straightforwardly determined.

Black women are doubly subordinated through relations of sexual and racial oppression, but it is by no means clear from the academic literature what that double subordination means in terms of their consciousness. The analysis of racial and sexual (as well as class) domination has tended to be carried out in parallel rather than in harness. Consequently, there has been little consideration of the ways in which sexual and racial oppression articulate in the formation of consciousness. I think it is fair to say that until very recently double subordination has been treated using a simple additive model. Thus Milner (1975) implicitly assumes that class and racial subordination operate in the same direction both inside and outside school, so that black working-class people are subordinated in essentially the same way as their white counterparts, but to class subordination should be added that based on 'race'/colour. Thus differences between white and black in the working class are ones of degree rather than of kind.

Such a model lacks specificity. More recent work (Clarricoates, 1980; Llewellyn, 1980) suggest that the interaction of double subordination (in both instances based on sex and class) may have contradictory not complementary (additive) effects, at least for girls; and, additionally, the contradictory nature of double subordination is expressed in different forms in differing contexts. Because, sociologically speaking, we still know so little about women, it is not possible to say whether the additive model is just too simple, whether it only applies to males, or is appropriate only where results for males and females are aggregated into one category.

It has long been known that, in social science research, to include females has risked destroying the theory and, in many cases, for that reason alone – that women 'don't fit' – females are excluded either at the sampling or analysing stage of research (Acker, 1980). If women generally have been a headache for social scientists it is part of the conventional wisdom that black women specifically are especially out of line with theoretical expectations (for example, black women are thought to find less difficulty in getting work than do men). Attempts have been made to explain this 'special' position of black women and I shall return to these later in the chapter. Mostly, these attempts have left the theories unchallenged and this is where the new studies (for example, Clarricoates, 1980; Kuhn and Wolpe, 1978; Llewellyn, 1980; MacDonald, 1980) are so important – they move us on conceptually. From having been ignored or relegated to an irritating and unexamined phenomenon the 'problem' of women is beginning to be theorised. This discussion of a black girls' subculture is offered as part of that endeavour.

The black girls were in their final year of compulsory schooling when the study began, attending a ten-form entry, mixed comprehensive in the London borough of Brent. The full study, involving white British, Asian (that is, of Indian or Pakistani parentage), and black (that is, of West Indian parentage) pupils of both sexes is described fully elsewhere (Fuller, 1978). In the following account, names have been changed to preserve anonymity. (I would like to thank the pupils and staff of the school concerned.)

Within the fifth year at Torville School, nearly a quarter of the pupils were black, a further one in four were Asian and just over half were white and British-born. For teaching purposes, the year was divided into parallel bands, the smaller containing pupils following a mixed practical/vocational/academic curriculum and in which white British and Asian boys were over-represented. I worked with the 'academic' band, where the majority of black pupils were British-born. (For a more comprehensive discussion of the methodology see Fuller, 1978). Although I focused on a small and particular group, the study is informed by constant comparisons with other same-age pupils in the school – male and female, Asian, white and black – all of whom were studied over a period of two years, for much of that time by intensive participant-observation. In our present state of ignorance concerning girls' subcultures generally, and those of black girls specifically, there is no way of adequately assessing how representative are the black girls at Torville School. They are located in the social formation in exactly the same way as other black women, but until we know more from black women themselves or from other forms of research, it is impossible to judge whether their response to double subordination is typical.

Most of the girls lived in two-parent families and some in mother-headed families; all had at least one brother or sister living with them and, in most cases, considerably more than one. Most mothers were permanently employed outside the home in full-time jobs. All the fathers were normally in permanent full-time employment. The girls came from predominantly working-class homes.

The subculture was school-based only in the limited sense that the girls were united in striving for academic qualifications, but it was neither a subculture of resistance to school nor of conformity to school. In terms of their expressed values and behaviour in school the girls manifested contradictory aspects of the good and bad pupil stance as these are described by others (Hargreaves, 1967; Lacey, 1970; Lambert, 1976; Werthman, 1971; Willis, 1977). To understand these contradictions and the particular meanings which academic achievement had for the girls, it is vital to look beyond the school to the situation of women and of ethnic minorities in the social formation. This the girls did consciously when discussing themselves and others in the group. In addition, they drew on their knowledge of the West Indies, knowledge based in many cases on personal experience and for all of them on close contact with people returning from visits. It is the girls' awareness of racism and sexism in Britain and the inferences which they drew concerning themselves as females in Caribbean society which provide the basis of the subculture and its values and particular style.

Within the fifth year, there was considerable unanimity between teachers' and pupils' definitions of the good and bad pupils. Good pupils were those who demonstrated their seriousness of purpose by certain kinds of classroom behaviour – attempting work set, punctuality, a modicum of attention to lesson content and a respectful (by no means always deferential) attitude towards teachers. The absence or opposite of this behaviour was read by teachers and pupils as indicating a lack of interest in school and was associated with a reputation as a 'bad' pupil.

In terms of classroom behaviour, the black girls gave all the appearances of being disaffected. Along with many pupils they viewed school as 'boring', 'trivial', 'childish'; their intolerance of the daily routines and their criticisms of much that went on inside the school were marked. They displayed a nicely judged insouciance for most aspects of the good pupil role; eschewing behaviour which would bring them into serious conflict with teachers, the girls were nevertheless frequently involved in activities which irritated or exasperated the staff. They neither courted a good reputation among teachers, nor seemed to want to be taken seriously by staff or other pupils. For example, it was easy to be misled into believing that the girls were not working in class when careful observation showed otherwise. Their stance towards school was puzzling for teachers and pupils for, despite what has been said, the girls did not automatically define teachers as adversaries, nor did they assume that school was irrelevant.

In ways which were more hidden to direct observation and which became clear only gradually through discussions and interviews with the girls away from the classroom, the girls were strongly committed to education and some aspects of schooling.

Alone among the fifth-formers some of the girls identified with certain teachers in the sense of admiring and wanting to emulate them. Beverley admired Miss Gaskell, 'Because she's a careers woman. She succeeded in life at a time in her days when women were expected to sit around ... she rebelled against that and she's got what she wanted, got her own car, got her own flat, completely independent, goes where she likes when she likes, she's got her own money, you know she's well paid. And now she's succeeded and got what she wants out of life, she's getting married – everything has kind of worked out for her.'

The girls were committed to achievement through the job market (Ladner, 1971) to a much greater degree than other girls. The differences lay not so much in the type of jobs they hoped to obtain, but rather in the resoluteness concerning their future work and in their certainty that whatever their future domestic circumstances they would want to be employed. During an interview Michelle said: 'I want a proper job first and some kind of skill so that if I do get married and have children I can go back to it; don't want just relying on him for money, cause I've got to look after myself, there must be something I can do.'

These are sentiments echoed by Monica: 'I should go out to work because, really, if I don't start learning to get on with it, I maybe will just have to leave home, get married and depend on the husband and I don't want that at all. ... Maybe I'll be a housewife or something like that, but I always picture myself working.'

The girls hoped to obtain 'good' jobs (within the restrictions of traditional women's work) and talked of the need to be 'ambitious' if they were to avoid unemployment or dead-end jobs. The high value they placed on education and educational qualifications as a necessary preparation for work was consciously related to their knowledge of high local and national unemployment levels and of the distinct possibility that they would encounter sexual and racial discrimination. It may be a simple measure of valuing education for its own sake but seems more likely to be part of their attempts to side-step discrimination that all the black girls remained in full-time education for at least one year beyond the statutory school-leaving age (few boys did). Where, at about 17, girls had left to take up work all mentioned that they were continuing their studies (by block or day-release schemes or by evening classes).

During their fifth year, not only were the girls confident that there was much they could do to avoid job discrimination, they were also confident of their ability to achieve the academic qualifications integral to their plans. At least by the time the study was complete, their optimism seemed well founded in that they had obtained a mean of 7·6 passes in O-level and CSE (compared with a mean of 5·6 for the black boys in the academic band) and, generally, with creditable grades. Only Asian boys achieved better results, as a group.

In barest outline, then, these are the major features of the subculture – a group of black girls at one and the same time apparently disaffected from schooling yet seemingly in their successful pursuit of paper qualification locked into an uncritical acceptance of a conventional justification of schooling. With the exception of Lambert's (1976) description of the Sisterhood (a group of younger girls in a single-sex grammar school) this particular conjunction of academic attainment and non-conformity to the rules, regulations and routines of school has not been described before.

I want to analyse this further: first in terms that the girls themselves used when discussing their posture in school and, secondly, in relation to certain themes that emerged from extensive interviews and less formal discussions.

To be viewed as 'good' pupils was inconsistent with the girls' own view of themselves, for such pupils were boring, unable to have fun and were, in other respects, immature. To behave in class like them would invite comparison with those from whom the black girls expressly distanced themselves. The girls believed that other pupils who 'had ambitions' placed too great an emphasis on teachers' opinions in relation to pupils' success in public examinations. They argued that success in externally marked exams depended on the quality of their work rather than on the quality of their relationship with those who taught them.

It is clear why, holding such views, the girls would give little priority to courting a good reputation at school. But there was another reason. In showing too much eagerness in class or appearing to take school too seriously, the black girls thought they risked the discovery by others of their academic and job ambitions; they believed this invited ridicule, and possibly more, from their black male peers: 'I find that most boys do have ambitions but they're influenced by their friends so they never get put into practice anyway. I think the girls are more ambitious but if they want to do something they don't feel embarrassed about it except when boys, when they hear you're doing O-levels, they won't come out with it and say you're a snob but they treat you a bit differently and you can feel it. ....'

It should not be thought that the experience and fear of ridicule by boys is limited to black girls. Shaw (1980) argues that it is a fact of life for girls in school to be the butt of boys' abuse and scorn, especially the nearer they come to challenging male dominance. Both she and Coleman (1961) point out the result of this – the girls either withdrawing from the competition or adopting various dissembling strategies. Their classroom behaviour can be seen as a conscious smokescreen to confuse others and enable the black girls at Torville School to retain the friendship of their peers (especially black boys) without having to lower their aspirations regarding education and employment.

Marcia described the pressures from the boys in the following way: 'I've always got my head in a book. I don't think they [boys in school] like it because they always commenting on it and they say, "You won't get anywhere", and sometimes I think they don't want me to learn or something like that, you know, but I spoke to my mum about it, and she said I shouldn't listen and I should keep working hard.'

These are the immediate explanations offered by the girls but, in themselves, they do not indicate why they were suspicious of male peers, how they arrived at their independence from adult's assessments of them and what academic qualifications meant to them. The girls' own explanations can be contextualised from interviews in terms of their experiential knowledge of sexual and racial subordination.

Domestic commitments (cleaning, cooking, child care, and so on) absorbed considerable amounts of the girls' time out of school. In common with many of the Asian and white girls interviewed, the black girls expressed considerable resentment that their brothers were not expected to undertake domestic tasks (either at all or to the same extent). This 'favouritism' was patently a source of considerable friction between girls and their parents, as well as between girls and their brothers. Yet, paradoxically, the discrepancy in demands made on girls and boys seemed to be one of the reasons for the girls' greater confidence in their ability – they were inclined to the view that boys were not asked to do these tasks because they were unable or incompetent, an interpretation all the more plausible because it echoed the division of competence, as they perceived it, between their parents in the home: ' . . . my dad helps around the house, he only helps with the good things – he never does the washing up . . . She's a lot better than my dad at things – he's good at the theory, but not on practical things'.

From accounts by both sexes, boys enjoyed both greater freedom of movement away from the home and greater freedom from domestic chores. This sexual division of labour was a source of both resentment and pride for the girls, a response which drew them more firmly into the 'feminine' sphere, but left them sceptical of the negative associations usually attached to female tasks.

The girls thought of themselves as capable, intelligent and the equals of boys, but were equally certain that this was not given sufficient public recognition: 'I think people trust you more when you're a boy, they say you're more reliable, you're more trustworthy. Because my dad always says that, he says you can take a boy and you can show him a trade, but you can take a girl and the next minute their heads are filled up with boys, that she just doesn't want to know. So I'm going to show him, you see!'

With amused disbelief most of the girls said they thought boys considered themselves superior to girls: ' . . . most West Indian boys definitely aren't going to let a woman dominate them or tell them what to do, they firmly believe they're the boss and she has to do everything . . . They just have this thing that they are the superior ones and women are inferior.'

Although they knew their own worth they believed this was often denied and it is here that the pursuit of educational qualifications takes on its special meaning – they did not need qualifications to prove their worth to themselves, but rather as a public statement of something which they already knew about themselves but which they were certain was not given sufficient recognition. This denial was evident within their own family and among their male peers; female peers were one source of confirmation.

Moving away from their daily experience of relations of sexual domination, it is possible to trace the girls' understanding that such relations exist throughout the social formation of Britain and the Caribbean. From experience, or others' accounts, they had built up a picture of a physically demanding, financially unrewarding life for women in the West Indies (a view shared by women in Foner's 1979 study). In comparison, men's lives were seen as pleasanter and less ardous, even given high unemployment. Return to the West Indies featured prominently in the boys' thoughts about the future. But the girls did not easily envisage a future for themselves in the West Indies; their awareness of their Caribbean roots led them to believe that, on balance, they would be materially better off in Britain. This is not to suggest that the girls dissociated themselves from their Caribbean origins or rejected themselves as blacks – they quite clearly did neither of these.

The conjunction of their positive identity as blacks but knowledge of racial discrimination in Britain, their positive identity as female but belief that in Britain and the Caribbean women were often accorded less than their due, meant that the girls were angry at the foreclosing of options available to them. This might be supposed to engender apathy and despair whereas, in practice, it elicited persistence and resourcefulness, as the following account shows:

> When I first went for the job I was very crafty when I wrote the letter, I put that I was a student and they thought I was coming from university and I did it in perfectly good English so they wouldn't think it was a foreign person. And then when I went and they actually saw that I was coloured I think they were a bit shocked, so they kept stalling and said come back tomorrow. They said the person isn't in, can you come back next week, and I wouldn't give in. Every time they said come back I'd go back and I'd go back. My dad was backing me all the way and in the end I got through.

Persistence, struggle and resourcefulness seem to be common themes among writers about black women (see, for example, Ladner, 1971), but it is as well to remember that this is not some expression of a cultural trait; rather, if the girls in this study are at all typical, it is a statement about the continuing double subordination of black women (see Prescod-Roberts and Steele, 1980).

The subculture emerged from the girls' positive acceptance of the fact of being female and black. They came together through each of them trying to cope with the difficulties of proving their own worth, especially as girls. Acute awareness of their double subordination was accompanied by a refusal to accept the 'faces' of subordination for themselves. The subculture's particular flavour stems from the girls' critical rejection of the negative connotations which the categorisation 'black' and 'female' commonly attracts. The girls' forms of action in school need to be understood as strategies for trying to effect some control over their present and future lives. Their analysis of the situation seemed to indicate the need for a programme of 'going it alone'. Their belief that secrecy was essential in this had an isolating effect, in the sense that within the classroom there was none of the visible solidarity which is typical of some school-based subcultures of boys; outside the classroom only that very small number of people 'in the know' could provide support. Confirmation of the girls' sense of identity could come neither from their general peer group nor from adults, but only from their own efforts. In short, this was a low-key, covert, rather than a celebratory, subculture of resistance.

In the final part of this chapter, I want to return to the theme of black women as in some way special, because different from white women. I shall take two recent studies of black girls' academic success (as judged against black boys' results in exams). In the earlier of these Driver (1977) argues that the girls' success can be attributed to the special support that the girls receive from their culture – specifically, encouragement from parents to strive at school. There is a suggestion that the girls are encouraged at the expense of boys, though it seems more likely (Tanner, 1974) that both sexes are encouraged, but the case of the girls is more noticeable to someone who takes lack of encouragement for girls as a given (that is, assumes sexism). Driver mentions that the girls in his study had heavy domestic commitments yet, in his analysis of conflicts between parents and children, the only conflict mentioned is between boys and their parents. It is not clear whether the girls (in striking contrast to those at Torville School) accepted these tasks without demur or whether they were not asked about conflict in this area because the sexual division of labour is unremarkable to the researcher. Whatever the reason, the effect is to suggest that girls have an easier time than boys in the family and that they inhabit a relatively privileged position there. Their 'privilege' and their academic success are to be understood as outcomes of living in a matriarchal culture (see also, Driver, 1979). The assumption that Afro-Caribbean societies are matriarchal is widespread and is based on such evidence as the central role of women as mothers in the kinship system, women's high rates of economic activity and the often-reported psychic strength of black women. In a matriarchy, by definition, women would not be subordinate because of their sex – they would have 'publicly recognised power and authority surpassing that of men' (Rosaldo and Lamphere, 1974, p. 3). There is no evidence that such a society exists in the Caribbean, and Tanner (1974) suggests the term 'matrifocal' better describes the important role of women in the family, which is nevertheless not generalised to power outside that institution.

A further look at the relationship between education, paid employment and power should clarify this point. The positive value placed on education among black parents needs first to be contextualised:

> The dream of a good education for their children has always had a particular significant for black people. White colonialists fed generations of Asians, Africans and West Indians the myth that the reason they were being savagely economically exploited was not because of race or class but because they were backward, under-developed, uneducated. The old colonialist equation of EDUCATION = POWER explains why so many black parents passionately wanted for their children the education they never had.... (Organisation of Women of Asian and African Descent, 1979, p. 6)

The power is, at least partly, conceived as obtaining better jobs than the parental generation. If girls receive encouragement in this process it is in recognition that they are likely to be breadwinners. Thus, Prescod-Roberts (1980), explicitly linking education with future earning power, suggests why girls in the West Indies may be supported by their family to pursue educational qualification. In a migratory economy, decisions have to be made as to who will reliably send remittances once they have migrated. She suggests that the sexual division of labour and responsibility within the family locks women more strongly and permanently into family responsibilities than it does men, and so makes women the better migrants from the perspective of those left behind. It is clear that such power as women obtain is directly channelled into the one institution in which women's power is sanctioned – the family.

So, even if the academic striving of the black girls at Torville School were to be understood as some form of 'cultural hangover' it can hardly be perceived as emanating from a culture in which the special place of women is one of privilege. In any case, it is not necessary to resort to culturalist explanations to make sense of the emphasis placed on paper qualifications by black girls at Torville School. It can be understood in two ways, both dependent on the effects of racial and sexual exclusion in Britain. The poor employment prospects and low wages which black males can command make it essential even in intact families for women to contribute financially to the family income – in a much higher proportion of cases than among whites, the black woman's wage is what pushes the family living standard above the poverty level. Thus, paid employment is not a choice for black women who cannot expect to rely on a husband's wage after marriage as some white women can. Related to this racial exclusion (which affects both black women and men even if black women can, as is sometimes suggested, get a job more readily than black men) it is important to recognise what sort of work this will be. As women, they will be excluded from all but the worst-paid, unskilled and semi-skilled work and paid at an even lower rate than men. To earn a living wage in such jobs requires working excessively long hours of overtime (which, in any case, are less likely to be made available to them as women). In these circumstances, the girl's pursuit of educational qualifications cannot be seen as some kind of individualistic self-improvement, but rather as a necessary strategy of survival.

The girls' strength and perseverance cannot be denied, but even if their ambitions are realised, they are not about to become part of a privileged élite. A labour market which is largely sex-segregated and which operates differential rates of pay for women and men means that the only edge which the black girls may have over black boys is that their paper qualifications may give them the option of obtaining their lower wages through shorter hours of work and in possibly more congenial working conditions.

Matrifocality can, and does, exist within essentially patriarchal social formations. I would argue that black women in Britain and the USA are faced with just such a situation. Matrifocality may allow women to develop with a definition of femininity that includes strength, competence and so which enables them to challenge patriarchal relations of sexual dominations, but it does not thereby do away with patriarchy.

Wilkinson argues that:

[Black] youth are unlike their white counterparts not only with respect to placement in the social structure and their definitions of the dynamics of inter-racial relations, but also with respect to the attitudinal orientation which emerges from their cultural experiences. They are different in the collective symbolism and self-oriented definitions of who they are and what they wish to become. For they must still contend with social issues that never confront white youth. (1975, p. 305)

Elaborating this theme, Miles and Phizacklea claim that 'it is the unique experience of blacks of racial exclusion that is the essence of black ethnicity' (1977, p. 495). As very much the same arguments can be made for women in relation to men, it is perhaps not surprising that the girls at Torville School were so conscious of sexual domination. That the double exclusion and domination should give rise to a positive sense of their worth among the black girls is interesting because it is not at all what would have been predicted from writings such as those by Fanon (1967) and Mitchell (1975). In a social formation characterised by racism and sexism it is not at all surprising that the black girls should have been finding it so difficult to have their sense of worth confirmed.

(I would like to thank Sandra Acker, Gill Boden and Jill Brown for their help in the preparation of this chapter)

7   The Debate on 'Sus'

BRIAN ROBERTS

The 1824 Vagrancy Act

An Act over 150 years old aimed at 'every suspected person or
reputed thief' has until recently been in force. Section 4 of the
Vagrancy Act 1824 prohibits 'every suspected person or reputed
thief frequenting any river, canal, or navigable stream, dock or
basin or any quay, wharf or warehouse near or adjoining thereto,
or any street, highway or avenue leading thereto, or any place of
public resort, or any avenue leading thereto, or any street or any
highway or any place adjacent to a street or highway with intent
to commit an arrestable offence.' The Criminal Attempts Act
came into force on 28 August 1981 and created a new offence of
'vehicle interference'.

The 1824 Act was meant to replace the previous complex
legislation on vagrancy leading back to medieval attempts to
regulate the supply and cost of labour following the decline in the
population due to the Black Death and later measures under the
Tudors to distinguish between the deserving and undeserving
poor in the provision of relief, punishment and work (Chambliss,
1964; Pound, 1971). The Act originally sought to control city
streets during a period of massive urban growth and an enormous
influx of wandering poor seeking work or merely the means of
staying alive. (For a discussion of how old laws can be used to new
ends, see Cashmore, 1978). This legislation was part of a concerted attempt, which included the formation of the Metropolitan
Police only five years later (1829) and the introduction of the New
Poor Law (1834) to maintain order among, what Marx called, 'the
reserve army of labour' and protect property, lines of communication and trade. Until recently, the application of this provision
against alleged 'suspected persons' or 'reputed thieves' appeared
to many critics to have the undesirable function of being used to
clear, arbitrarily, certain shopping centres and inner-city areas of
particular young people, especially young blacks. A great deal of
bitterness has resulted towards the police in their use of the
'being a suspected person' or 'sus' charge and the issue has
become inextricably part of a wider controversy regarding civil
liberties and the extent of police powers. Why is it, then, that the

police organisations and the Home Office believe that this old law (or a modified replacement) is not merely still needed but is also an important, if not vital, weapon against street crime?

It has been established by a number of court cases that a 'suspected person' or 'reputed thief' is a person who has already become the object of suspicion quite apart from the particular occasion immediately prior to arrest. Also the acts which cause an individual to be a suspected person and the act which causes the arrest need not be separated by any particular length of time (perhaps only a matter of seconds) so long as they are separate acts, and they need not be different in kind (*Halsbury's*, 1969; Leigh, 1975). A common 'sus' case is where it is alleged that an individual has paid unusual attention to shopping bags in a bus queue. The first example of this attention provides the identity of a 'suspected person', the second demonstrates the offence. The offence is a summary one which means that the defendant has no right to elect for jury trial. The present maximum penalty for first conviction is a fine of £100 and/or three months' imprisonment. On further conviction, the offender can be deemed an 'incorrigible rogue' and sent to the Crown Court for sentence with a maximum penalty of one year's imprisonment. Three aspects of the offence must be covered before an arrest can take place: the arrested person must be a 'suspected person' or 'reputed thief', must be loitering with intent to commit an arrestable offence (mere suspicious behaviour is not enough), and must be loitering in one of the public places named. Because the actions in question may be very close in time together it has been argued that a reduction has resulted in the distinction between the production of the status of 'suspected person' and the action causing arrest. An important danger may result in that the police may act against those who are loitering innocently, that is, without criminal intent (Leigh, 1975, p. 97). A further feature of the offence is that evidence often rests in court on the statements of two police officers without independent witnesses or the intended victim being brought forward.

The Runnymede Trust has recorded details of a large number of 'sus' cases. The following example gives an indication of the ease of conviction and the possible grave deficiencies in criminal procedure that are associated with the charge.

Four black youths were doing their Saturday morning shopping in Upton Park. They had just come out of Woolworths when they were stopped by a group of plain clothed policemen. One of them allegedly said he had seen the boys 'operating' the Saturday before. They were taken to Forest Gate Police Station, put in separate cells, stripped, searched and later questioned, photographed and had their fingerprints taken. They were charged with 'sus' – jostling people in bus and shop queues and putting their hands in shopping baskets. They denied the charges. In court the police were not sure whether one of the potential victims was black or white, could not describe the bag and disagreed over which hand she was holding it in. They failed to identify one of the defendants – one of them said that this choice was a 'guess' as 'all blacks look the same to me'. The police disagreed over whether or not the defendants had been stripped. There were no independent witnesses. But the manager of Woolworths gave evidence that the boys were not hanging around the tills, as alleged by the police. They were convicted. They appealed and the conviction was quashed because of discrepancies in the police evidence. (Demuth, 1978, pp. 22–3)

During 1976 in England and Wales 3,501 persons were charged with 'sus' resulting in 2,738 convictions. There were very interesting distributions according to sex, race and location to be found in 'sus' statistics. For instance, only 2 per cent of persons proceeded against for 'sus' were female, a surprisingly low figure when compared with the 16·1 per cent for females for 'theft from the person' proceedings in the same year. According to Demuth, 'most cases are brought by the police and the pattern of the offence appears to be determined by whether or not it is local police practice to use this particular charge'. She states that in 1976 'the Metropolitan Police District accounted for 1,914 charges (55 per cent of all charges brought); Merseyside 430 (12 per cent); Manchester 260 (7 per cent); West Midlands 167 (5 per cent); South Wales 148 (4 per cent) and West Yorkshire 82 (2 per cent). The rest of the country accounted for the remaining 15 per cent'. The discrepancies between areas becomes more obvious when the figures are related to the population of each area; for instance, according to the 1971 Census, Greater London had only 15 per cent of the population (but 55 per cent of the 'sus' charges). Some cities make little use of the charge, for example, the Bristol area had only seventeen prosecutions in 1976 (Demuth, 1978, pp. 36–7).

A survey by the Law Centres Federation (of cases they had dealt with) not only found marked differences between areas, but was able to identify exact locations where frequent arrests for the offence were made. It stated that the 'most likely place to get arrested is the W1 area of Central London, particularly Oxford Street and even more particularly the bus stops in Oxford Street. The next most likely places are W10 and especially Portobello Market, and the bus stops in Brixton Road' (Law Centres Federation, 1979, app., p. 8). While high 'sus' rates generally coincide with popular shopping areas, there does seem to be a concentration in the use of the offence in certain areas of South West and

West London. The Law Centres Federation concluded that it was striking that in some areas, such as Camden and Islington, there is little or no use of the charge. A frequent serious allegation made against the police is that they are racially biased in their use of the 'sus' charge. Some data is available on the ethnic background of 'sus' case arrests.

Metropolitan Police District figures collected for arrests in 1975 for 'sus' according to ethnic background showed that blacks 'constituted 40·4 per cent of all "suspected person" arrests and 37·1 per cent of all "other violent theft" (mainly handbag snatching) arrests. The proportions for robbery (28·7 per cent) and assault (20·7 per cent) were next highest, while for all other indictable crime arrests of blacks were 11·1 per cent of the total. The proportion of blacks in the population in the London MPD in 1975 was estimated to be 4·2 per cent' (Rees, Stevens and Willis, 1979, p. 11). In 1976, 2,112 persons were arrested in the MPD for 'sus'; blacks constituted 42 per cent of this figure. In 1977 44 per cent of 'sus' arrests were of black people and in 1978 43 per cent.

These figures on 'sus' clearly show that blacks are arrested far more frequently in relation to their numbers in the general population than whites. The police view is that the figures do not represent a bias against black youth but rather that the arrests for 'sus' reflect the relative involvement of various groups in that form of street crime. Presumably, if blacks arrested for 'sus' begins to decline (and in proportion to other groups) this merely shows their declining involvement rather than any change in police discretion or policy. (One London group, Haringey Community Relations Council, recently noted that the proportion of black people arrested for 'sus' declined from 47 per cent in 1977 to 10 per cent in 1978 of total arrests – Brent and Crawford, 1979.)

Police–Black Relations and Crime

The 'sus' issue must be seen within the context of the history of police–black relations to be understood fully. Not only has the use of the charge itself by the police created bitterness and resentment but also the issue has become a symbolic precis of the accumulation of the wide-ranging and serious criticisms that have been made against the police by the black community in recent years. The Institute of Race Relations, for example, has compiled from disparate sources a large number of incidents of alleged malpractice. The institute gives examples of the disregard of the Judges' Rules, the inadequate investigation of racial attacks, the abuse of the power to enter homes, pressure on juveniles to accept guilt and the saturation of areas by special units, such as the Special Patrol Group, where there is a high concentration of black people.

Currently, hostility and resentment towards the police is the outcome of a growing feeling throughout the 1960s and 1970s. Recent riots at Ladywood and Leicester following the activities of the National Front, and the disturbances at Notting Hill, Bristol, Brixton and elsewhere are the result of a longer-term experience. In 1971 a Select Committee of the House of Commons felt it necessary to examine rising complaints against the police and general concern regarding police–black relations. Both the black community and the police organisations gave evidence that the situation was bad between black youth and the police. Black organisations complained of harassment and intimidation while the police described certain sections of black youth as being an alienated group who had a distrust of the police. The Select Committee concluded that, 'it was made clear by all witnesses, police, Community Relations Councils and other bodies, but chiefly by West Indians themselves, that relations between the police and younger West Indians ... are fragile, sometimes explosive' (Select Committee on Race Relations and Immigration, 1971–2, Vol. 1., p. 69). The complaint of police discrimination was supported, around this time, by a 'survey' of police–black relations by Derek Humphry who concluded that 'the last ten to fifteen years have produced massive evidence to demonstrate that equality under the law is not a right Black people in the country would automatically expect' (Humphry, 1972, p. 233). His view that the problem was more than the result of minor aberrations in police practice was echoed by John Lambert in his study of Birmingham. Lambert argued that the professional role of the police officer is informed by wider social prejudices and may be expected to be 'no more or less prejudiced than their neighbours and equals' (J. Lambert, 1970, p. 181). But, he adds a significant qualification: the professional role of the police officer involves more contact with black people and so they have more opportunity for their prejudices to be reinforced and to act according to their feelings. Other, more recent writers have also argued that there is bias in the police treatment of blacks (Cain, 1973; Pulle 1973; Moore, 1975; Short, 1978; Hall *et al.*, 1978). This view has been challenged by James (1979) who argues that policing by lower ranks and their malpractices are aimed equally at black and white. However, his study appears to be rather dependent on a limited observation of a crime squad and a number of interviews with police officers. A controversial view of police–black relations and black involvement in crime has been given by John

Brown (1977) who gave a portrait of Handsworth in Birmingham as a community more or less at the mercy of two hundred quasi-Dreads who were even able to keep the crime rate down through intimidation of victims and witnesses. This rather emotive view of black crime was fiercely challenged by Cashmore (1979a, ch. 10) and Rex and Tomlinson (1979) who pointed out (from Brown's own figures) that Handsworth did not appear exceptional in crime rates and strongly doubted the existence of a tightly knit, well-organised and violent criminal subculture.

The police have always denied any bias against black people and have vigorously defended their use of the 'sus' charge. For instance, James Anderton, the Chief Constable of Greater Manchester, has stated strongly that his force was impartial in using the 'sus' charge and he described the offence as an 'unnecessarily controversial piece of legislation' (Anderton, 1979). The police argue that the disproportionate number of blacks in the 'sus' figures must be due to the greater involvement of black youths in the crime and so they will come more to the attention of the police than their numbers in the population at large would suggest. The connection between blacks and crime has been forged in statements by the police and others. Sir David McNee, the Commissioner of the Metropolitan Police, pointed out that 'law and order in the capital are now firmly linked to matters of race' (*Daily Mirror*, 19 June 1979). This link was also recognised by Enoch Powell at a rather earlier date when, following the 'mugging scare' of 1972–3, he put the race–crime equation rather differently by identifying 'mugging' as a characteristic black crime – a connection cemented by the National Front's racialist anti-'black muggers' campaign during past elections and subsequent highly publicised marches through areas of black residence (see Hall *et al.*, 1978).

Because of the concern regarding the race–crime issue and the lack of available data, the Home Office Research Unit began a detailed examination of the possible connection between ethnicity and arrest rates in 1975. After some difficulties and delay, possibly due to objections raised by the Metropolitan Police on the kinds of social factors to be considered (Mackie, 1978), this research has now been published (Rees, Stevens and Willis, 1979; Stevens and Willis, 1979). The first part of the study, which examined seven major conurbations, found that the incidence of recorded indictable crime in 1971 was not related to the proportion of ethnic minorities in those areas. Tyneside, for instance, with a high recorded arrest rate did not have the same proportion of West Indians in its population as London and the West Midlands. Even within conurbations this result was confirmed. In

London the study found that Camden and Tower Hamlets, with low proportions of West Indians, had higher recorded crime rates than areas with high proportions of West Indians, such as Lambeth and Hackney. It must be remembered that these results relate only to total indictable recorded crime and cannot be assumed for specific offences. In addition, they cannot answer the question whether West Indians or Asians are either under or over involved in indictable crime. The second part of the study was based on the Metropolitan Police District and drew upon its information gathered on the ethnic background of persons arrested. The differences between white, black and Asian arrest rates were largely statistically accounted for by various demographic and socio-economic factors, even so, for some offences – assault, robbery and other violent theft (especially the least serious examples of these offences) – blacks still appear to be disproportionately involved. A combination of intrinsic and extrinsic factors, the authors argued, may provide the answer.

> Evidence for intrinsic factors consists, on the one hand, of disproportionately high black and Asian unemployment ... and, on the other hand, of victims' reports of street offences ... Evidence for extrinsic factors lies in the fact that blacks are being most heavily arrested for two kinds of offence in which there is considerable scope for selective perception of potential or actual offenders; other violent theft (largely handbag snatching), and being a 'suspected person' under the provisions of the Vagrancy Act 1824, where the chances of being arrested were 14 or 15 times the white chances. These figures are so much higher than might be expected that they prompt the questions whether arrest rates accurately reflect the respective involvement of whites and blacks in criminal activity, and if not, whether the hypothesis that the suspicions of policemen bear disproportionately on blacks may account for some of the difference. (Stevens and Willis, 1979, p. 41)

The authors do not make any recommendations as to which explanation they favour,

> All that can be said with certainty is that the extent of total recorded indictable crime in any conurbation or police division is not related to the presence of ethnic minorities; that blacks were in the MPD (1975) arrested more frequently than whites; but that a large part of this excess can be statistically accounted for by the deprivations specific to the black, white, and Asian populations. These findings are important in the context of some current beliefs that there is a positive relationship between the presence of ethnic minorities and the general level of crime in an area. Finally, it has been found that while victims' reports and arrest rates point to the conclusion that blacks are excessively involved in recorded street crime, the data also suggest that blacks are

more liable to be picked up by the police (particularly 'suspected person' and other violent theft arrests). The latter findings, while not necessarily contradictory, are disturbing. (Ibid., pp. 41–2)

This very important research leaves open the possibility that blacks may be disproportionately involved in street crime. Given that blacks face a range of social disadvantages it would not be surprising that occasional crime may have some attraction to some groups. However, the research indicates that this would be only a very partial explanation of the disproportionate involvement of blacks in certain offences (according to arrest rates). The discretion or selective perceptions of police officers are more easily brought into play with regard to street crime. Those discussions of police–black relations which have pointed to police discrimination have, therefore, not been refuted by this research and have found possible strong support.

The 'Sus' Debate

The present debate on 'sus' can be traced back to the Home Office Working Party on Vagrancy and Street Offences appointed in 1971 by the then Home Secretary, Reginald Maudling, a decision which reflected the Conservatives' 'law and order' platform in the 1970 election in which they promised to review or alter a wide range of legislation. The Working Party was comprised overwhelmingly of Home Office and police representatives. Its interim *Working Paper* (Working Party, 1974) gave a firm indication of its thinking by arguing that the 'sus' charge should not be entirely abolished. It agreed with the argument given by the police that some kind of similar offence was required but saw no need to retain the category of 'reputed thief' which rested on previous bad character and previous convictions. The *Working Paper* argued,

> The criminal law requires too much evidence to support a charge of attempt for it to be possible to deal with all such criminal activity (i.e. activity which falls within the scope of 'sus') as attempted offences, even bearing in mind the possibility of an extension of the existing law on attempts ... The new offence might then refer to 'a course of suspicious conduct', or 'a repetition of suspicious conduct' or, by exclusion, provide that it should not suffice to establish suspicion that there has been only one instance of such conduct. (Working Party, 1974, pp. 59–60).

This view reinforces the police contention that the charge was necessary to maintain the efficient fight against crime, being applicable in those instances where the offender had not reached the point where the charge of attempt could be brought. Thus, it was deemed an essential aid to deterrence and the prevention of more serious offences as part of the vital need to defend the streets from the rising amount of crime. Although the government expressed acceptance of the Working Party's *Report* (1976) the recommendation on 'being a suspected person' has not been introduced. The report noted that the interim recommendations of the Working Party (in the *Working Paper*) had met with some strong support but also opposition in terms of the charge of 'sus' being a 'convenience law' since it applied more to the possibility of an offence rather than the commission of definite criminal action. The report maintained, following the *Working Paper*, that despite other suggestions the maximum punishment for the offence should be a fine and/or three months' imprisonment and that it should not be triable by jury.

In response to the criticisms of the *Working Paper*, including those in the National Council for Civil Liberties' *Vagrancy: An Archaic Law* (1975), regarding the vagueness of the offence and the nature of the evidence required, the *Report* stated: 'We recognise that some criticism of our proposals stems from the view that an offence of being suspected of being about to commit a serious offence in a public place is open to abuse, and lays the police open to allegations of abuse when they invoke it. Nevertheless we think that there are situations where society has a right to be protected in which a person is apparently embarking on a criminal project' (Working Party, 1976, p. 15). According to the NCCL, 'the evidence is invariably given by police officers only. Because by definition no substantive theft, or even sufficient proximate act to charge an attempted theft, takes place the question for the court becomes one of interpretation of a few actions which may or may not indicate an intent' (NCCL, 1975, p. 8). A more detailed legal examination of 'sus' was made by Leigh, who regarded vagrancy and other status offences as posing grave problems for civil liberties: 'A number of dangers are involved. One is that arrests will take place on the basis of little evidence; far less than would suffice for an attempt. Another is that extensive powers may well be used for the purpose of harassing known petty offenders. Situations are defined as offences whereas in substance the situation is simply such that the commission of an offence, ultimately, seems very probable' (Leigh, 1975, p. 103).

A very important step in the debate on 'sus' was the formation of the Scrap Sus Campaign by community workers and others in 1978. The realisation of the use of the charge and its difficulties for the defendant, stemming from increasing evidence from legal and community centres, brought about efforts to not only abolish the charge but to call for an independent inquiry into police–black relations. An important feature of this campaign, apart from making the discussion of the offence wider than merely in legal circles, was the very active involvement of a large number of black parents in the organisation and at public meetings. This broad support in the black community enabled the campaign to enlist some political backing from MPs. In December 1978 the Liberal Peer, Lord Avebury, introduced the Suspected Persons (Abolition) Bill in the House of Lords. The measure received support from Lords Gardiner, Gifford, Pitt, and others but failed to gain a Second Reading being thrown out by thirty-two votes to eighty-two. In the debate, Lord Gardiner, a former Lord Chancellor, pointed out that 'a man of unblemished character can be sent to prison for three months without right of trial by jury, when he has not committed any criminal offence and cannot even be convicted of an attempt to commit a criminal offence, merely because there is evidence that he intends to do so' (Gardiner, 1978). Lord Harris, Minister of State at the Home Office, said that the government accepted the recommendations of the Working Party on Vagrancy and Street Offences that there should be a more modern provision substituted for the offence but until that could be done the charge should remain as a valuable weapon in the police armoury. In the House of Commons at the beginning of 1979 Labour MPs, Jo Richardson, Arthur Latham and John Tilley put down an Early Day Motion to gauge support for repeal but only forty-two signatures were received.

The police maintain that any abuses in their use of the 'sus' charge are exceptional and that the charge is not unusual according to legal criteria and so does not merit special attention or debate. They still do not seem to realise, at least in official pronouncements, the widespread and deep hostility towards the use of the offence of 'being a suspected person' which has been aroused in the black community. Many black people attending local meetings (often containing several hundred people) organised by the Scrap Sus Campaign have declared that simply being young, black and on the street appears to be sufficient 'evidence' for police action on many occasions. The damage done to police–black relations, as well as criticism in legal terms, have been strongly emphasised by black organisations. These views were put forward in detail to the Royal Commission on Criminal Procedure which reported in January 1981. The Scrap Sus Campaign stated in its memorandum to the Royal Commission that this particular legislation 'is the single most important cause of the deteriorating relationship between the police and young black people' (Scrap Sus Campaign, 1979, p. 55). The campaign placed its discussion of the charge within the context of the history of black subordination and current disadvantage and recommended (in addition to the abolition of 'sus') a whole series of changes in police training and local accountability. Although the Royal Commission's terms of reference were aimed at a broader level of police powers and responsibilities (for example, arrest and interrogation procedures), citizen's rights and duties and prosecution procedure, the specific charge of 'sus' figured prominently in written evidence submitted to it. (However, not from police organisations whose views on the charge have largely been given through public speeches.) A very diverse range of social welfare, religious, civil rights and race organisations, including the NCCL, the National Council for Social Service, the Law Centres Federation, the Catholic Commission for Racial Justice, the British Council of Churches, the National Youth Bureau and the Institute of Race Relations, called for the repeal of the charge. In addition, editorials in the *Guardian* (30 December 1978) and *New Society* (22 March 1979) have opposed the offence.

The general view of these groups was that the charge should not be merely amended, as called for by the Home Office Working Party on Vagrancy and Street Offences, because any such alteration would quite likely have the same unsatisfactory features, that is, the lack of independent witnesses, the vagueness of the idea of suspicious behaviour and the difficulty in assessing intent, and the scope for abuse by police officers wishing to harrass young black people or other groups. It has also been noted recently that these same criticisms were made against the 'sus' law when it was used against the unemployed in city areas during the 1930s (Scaffardi, 1980; NCCL, 1975; McNee, 1980). The existence of this kind of law, it is argued, can only undermine the acceptance of police impartiality; the possibilities for arbitrary application and the ease of conviction it provides and can only further worsen police–black relations by creating resentment towards the police. Several submissions to the Royal Commission pointed to the fear or distrust that many young blacks (and young whites) had in encounters with the police on the street or the police station. The National Youth Bureau, for example, stated that there was fear of the consequences of being known to have a criminal record and that young people (from their evidence) consistently pointed to the use of 'sus' as an area of police malpractice (National Youth Bureau, 1979).

The two surveys already mentioned of 'sus' usage were also

submitted. The Law Centres Federation drew upon cases dealt with by its constituent organisations in 1978. The survey covered a total of 207 defendants charged with 'sus'; in these cases blacks comprised over double (87 per cent) the figures officially given previously for black involvement in 'sus' in the Metropolitan District (for arrests). While this difference can probably be accounted for by a possible bias in their sample perhaps it is less easy to explain the very wide discrepancies in the use of the charge they uncovered between various police areas – even areas with similar ethnic and socio-economic backgrounds. A very influential survey by Clare Demuth for the Runnymede Trust (originally published in 1978) was also presented to the Royal Commission. This independent piece of research was based on information from 170 'sus' cases involving 299 defendants. She also noticed that certain locations were frequent sites for 'sus' arrests. In addition, she found that there were, in effect, two kinds of 'sus' – the first usually involves tampering with car-door handles and young whites are overwhelmingly picked up by the police for this type, the second involves intent to 'pickpocket' or 'handbag snatch' and here the police direct their attention (disproportionately) to black youth. Demuth concluded that there were a number of cases of obvious abuse of the charge but that it was difficult to ascertain how indiscriminate the police were in the use of the 'sus' law. Where cases of abuse arose it seemed that the police were mainly concerned with 'asserting their control over the blacks on the streets than with niceties of being certain that the youth in question was intending to commit an offence at the moment when he was arrested' (Demuth, 1978, p. 53).

While the police preferred to follow the general guidelines offered by the Royal Commission for the submission of evidence (covering police powers and duties and details of prosecution procedure), rather than submit a discussion of the specific charge of 'sus', they have commented on organisations favouring abolition through their press campaign. Sir David McNee has accused church bodies of 'meddling' in police matters when they criticise police methods of dealing with street crime (*Guardian*, 24 August 1979). Jim Jardine of the Police Federation sees church and welfare organisations as being 'conned' by the 'protest industry' into believing allegations against the police which have no basis in fact (Jardine, 1979). Unlike the police, the Home Office did give evidence on 'sus' as part of 'background material' on ethnic minorities' and young peoples' relations with the police. Its conclusion appeared to be that it still supported its own Working Party on Vagrancy and Street Offences Report and, in addition, it did not believe that changes in the 'sus' law would 'necessarily of themselves have any effect on police relations with the community' (Home Office, 1979, p. 13). Unfortunately, it did not examine the criticisms of the offence in detail or discuss the work of its own Research Unit (now being cut in size) on the relation between ethnicity and crime.

A high point was reached in the campaign against 'sus' with the recommendation by the Home Affairs Committee of the House of Commons (which had been taking evidence on race relations and 'sus') in May 1980 that the offence should be abolished without delay (Home Affairs Committee, 1980). The committee of six Conservative and five Labour MPs cited the now very familiar criticisms of the offence but in a debate in Parliament William Whitelaw, the Home Secretary, fended off an Opposition motion calling for immediate repeal by arguing that while the government was in favour of abolition, a new offence was required to fill the 'real loophole in the law of attempt' which would be left. (*Guardian*, 6 June, 1980). The Opposition motion to note the Home Affairs Committee's report with approval was rejected by 283 votes to 228. Instead, a government amendment was accepted which effectively postponed the repeal of 'sus' until 'the imminent publication of the Law Commission's report on Attempt and ... the public response to these, as providing the basis for an early decision as to the best way of reforming the law while ensuring adequate protection for the public' (Muchlinsky, 1980, p. 152). A few months later (on 6 August) the committee took the very unusual step of publishing a further short report on 'sus' again recommending abolition, having been alarmed by the debate and the subsequent speeches by various Home Office ministers. The members argued that 'sus' had acquired a symbolic significance in representing the difficult relations between blacks and the police and that its abolition would help to improve that relation. (Jill Knight was the lone dissenting voice on the Committee.) Repeal would not leave a significant gap in police powers and, in any case, the police could intervene to protect the public in various other ways. It concluded that it did not want to see 'sus' replaced by similar offences dressed in more modern language. Such attempts at 'verbal cosmetics' would not be welcome; instead, the report stated that the repeal of 'sus' would signify 'the removal of a piece of law which is contrary to the freedom and liberty of the individual'. In arguing so strongly against 'sus' laws, the committee were certainly challenging the unswerving support given for the offence by the police in their evidence and the earlier reforms proposed by the Home Office. The Commission for Racial Equality, in their submission to the committee, seemed to want more research to be undertaken before making up its mind, while the Home Office tended to leave the question open (as it did in evidence to the Royal Commission on Criminal Procedure) (Mackie, 1980). However, an indication of Home Office thinking had been given by William Whitelaw in a speech on 11 July (in response to the Law Commissions proposals on attempt) which had led the committee to believe (accurately as it has turned out) that an offence was to be introduced which was specifically related to tampering with motor vehicles. If this was true, the committee stated that such a new law would extend the criminal law on intent and it called on the government to say 'clearly and unequivocally' if 'sus' was to be re-enacted, and also stated that doubts concerning the effect of repeal were unfounded. The committee noted the urgency of the situation and demanded that a clear understanding should be given that legislation was to be introduced to repeal 'sus' in the following parliamentary session. A further surprise was given by the chairperson of the committee, John Wheeler, MP for Paddington, in presenting the report. He stated that if the Queen's Speech did not mention the repeal of 'sus', the unprecedented step of tabling a Private Member's Bill signed by the committee or finding an individual MP to put a Bill would be made (Mackie, 1980). In reply to this challenge and, of course, as a result of longer-term developments in Home Office policy in the area, the Queen's Speech did mention 'sus'; however, the offence was not to be totally abolished but replaced by one relating to motor vehicles based on the common law of attempt.

The result of Home Office deliberations was the Criminal Attempts Bill (published in December 1980) which sought to redefine the law of attempt and replace 'sus' by a new offence of interfering with a motor vehicle in a public place without the owner's consent or lawful authority (with a maximum penalty of three months' in prison or a £500 fine, or both). The law of attempt was to be defined as involving something more than a mere preparation with intent to commit a crime. A person would be guilty of an offence even though technically the crime was impossible; for instance, picking a pocket which was empty. But a person would not be guilty if the intended result was not an offence; for instance, handling 'stolen goods' which were not in fact stolen. The NCCL, among others, immediately pointed out the continued dangers within the new Bill. The offence of inter-ference was unnecessary and the onus of proof was on those who sought to implement a new offence to justify it; 'trivia' was being introduced into the criminal law (*Guardian*, 20 December 1980, p. 2). According to the *Guardian* the repeal of the 'sus' law was a forward step but the offence of 'interference' had certain familiar dangers, 'at present, it is said to be hard to decide precisely what offence someone trying a car door handle intends to commit. So "interfering" with a car will itself become an offence – subject to proof of the offender's intentions. This could lead to a repetition of the very abuses that produced the overwhelming calls for the abolition of "sus". True, intention by itself will no longer be a crime. But intention will still have to be proved' (*Guardian*, editorial, 20 January 1981) The editorial agreed with the statement made by the Home Affairs Committee on 'sus', 'we are satisfied that it is not in the public interest to make behaviour interpreted as revealing criminal intent, but equally open to innocent interpretation, subject to criminal penalties' (*Guardian*, editorial, 20 January 1981). As Roy Hattersley, the Shadow Home Secretary, pointed out in the Second Reading of the Bill (19 January), the new offence would still rest on one person's judgement on what was taking place in another person's mind and supported the Home Affairs Committee's criticisms of the 'sus' charge. In addition, he asked why if the charge was so essential, some police forces never used it. Nevertheless, William Whitelaw still argued that a new offence was required to 'plug the gap' and while the use of the offence had undoubtedly had a detrimental effect on police relations with ethnic minorities, the Home Affairs Committee had not found any evidence that the Metropolitan Police had used it with a deliberate racial bias (again overlooking the Home Office's own research) (*Guardian*, 20 January, 1981). While it appears, at first sight, that the Bill abolishes 'sus', even the *Police Review* commented that the Bill was 'conceived in haste' and 'gives the police a wider power of arrest than they ever wanted' (*State Research Bulletin*, 1981, p. 70). The new substantive offence, still only triable in magistrates courts, gives a constable the power to arrest without warrant anyone who with 'reasonable cause' he suspects may be guilty of the 'interference offence'. According to *Police Review*, 1981, this power could easily result in officers interpreting '"reasonable cause" in a manner calculated to produce nervous breakdowns'. At the very least, the Bill gives plenty of scope for the kind of street harrassment like that found under the old 'sus' law (*State Research Bulletin*, 1981, p. 70).

The Police and the Community

A common recommendation in the evidence given to the Royal Commission by organisations calling for the abolition of 'sus' was that the police should become more conscious of the longer-term effects of some of their actions on community relations. In addition, there are calls for a more systematic and sensitive programme of police education on ethnic minorities and for the movement away from the unnecessary use of strong-arm tactics which create a common hostility towards the presence of the police (as witnessed at Southall) and for such measures to be strictly regulated and limited to exceptional circumstances. It is very unfortunate that the outside intervention of groups like the Special Patrol Group into an area can dramatically end any tentative steps towards mutual trust and co-operation which may have been built up between the police and local groups.

What we have seen, especially in recent years, is an increasing division of labour within the police which has resulted on occasion in some of its roles (in particular, those represented by welfare or community policing and the para-military specialist units) coming into conflict due to differences in the theoretical premisses and practical application of various kinds of policing. This contradiction and the possible effects on community relations have been recognised quite clearly by some senior police officers. Mr Dear, the Assistant Chief Constable of Nottinghamshire, has candidly said of the work of his force's Special Control Unit, 'They might apparently solve one problem, but in its wake create another of aggravated relationships between minority groups and the police in general. It is in this atmosphere that the permanent beat officer is expected to continue his work – often finding that his task, which has always been difficult and delicate, has now been made almost impossible (Whitaker, 1979, p. 68). John Alderson (1979), the Chief Constable of Devon and Cornwall, has become well known for his ideas on 'community policing' and his warning that there are dangers in the shift, as he sees it, from an older style of preventative policing towards a more militaristic mode. He told a conference of European police chiefs and advisers: 'The modern generation of police officers are beginning to see themselves as mobile responders to incidents. Technology is seductive. The car, radio and the computer dominate the police scene. The era of preventative policing is phasing out in favour of a responsive or reactive police ... The technological cop has arrived' (Cranfield Papers, 1979, pp. 14–15).

However, some caution must be exercised before such a view can be accepted; not only may the traditional 'preventative' account of police practice in British police history be overdrawn but an alternative view of the apparent contradiction in modern policing functions can be posed. There is still, no matter what approach is pursued, a central concern and duty by the police to deal with crime. Specific or localised contradictions remain within the unifying function of crime control. In this light, the preventative community policing or community-relations policy, as in John Alderson's 'consensual paternalism', is a means of surveillance and intelligence gathering in the crime war by a closeness to the community which a technological approach, by itself, lacks. Community policing must be welcomed but there are dangers for the community which may arise. At its worst, as in times of social conflict and division, 'low-level' policing can be used directly as an arm of the security services for data gathering on every aspect of the lives of certain sections of the community, as in Northern Ireland. It is worth noting at this point that there has arisen something of a 'Dixon of Dock Green myth' in the history of British policing. The consensual nature of British policing has a history but there is also, another, more outwardly repressive, story to be written (compare Ascoli, 1979, with Bunyan, 1977). There is also an important irony here regarding preventative policing; the 'sus' law can be viewed as a preventative measure *par excellence* as the argument for its retention rests on the idea that it is better to intervene before a serious crime is committed. Indeed, it could be said that 'prevention' as originally meant in the Vagrancy Act was the 'controlling' of the streets by clearing away, if necessary, undesirable characters. In much the same way, the massive use of stop and search and the aggressive or reactive function of special units have been defended under the definition of prevention. While John Alderson's advocacy of 'community policing' may be applauded there remain dangers with his conception, particularly with the definition of what constitutes the 'community leadership' role of the police upon which he rests his whole approach and his resistance to police accountability (*State Research Bulletin*, 1980, pp. 65–7).

Apart from the reservations regarding the use of specialist units made by John Alderson and some other senior police officers, the police response to criticism has so far been disappointing, indeed the triumvirate of McNee, Anderton and Jardine have singled such units out for praise. Sir David McNee's stout defence of the SPG is well known. He told a black reporter at a press conference following statements by witnesses implicating the group in the death of Blair Peach at Southall anti-National Front protest: 'If you keep off the streets of London and behave yourselves you won't have the SPG to worry about. I understand the concern of your people. But if you don't get into trouble you won't come into confrontation with the police' (*Guardian*, 15 June, 1979). (A similar comment has recently been made by Sir Robert Mark on the death of Blair Peach.) It is worth comparing this statement with the view of the Institute of Race Relations (IRR):

> The SPG ... has been increasingly deployed in so-called 'high-crime' areas (Brixton, Peckham, Lewisham, Tooting, Stoke Newington, Kentish Town, Hackney and Notting Hill), which are in reality decaying inner city areas of substandard housing, low amenities and high unemployment where the white working class and the majority of black people live. Evidence of its operations in these areas clearly demonstrates that black people have been a prime target of the SPG, especially in Lewisham and Lambeth. The tactics used by the SPG, officers when 'doing-over' a 'high-crime' area are aggressive (because of their training in riot control), result in a high proportion of arrests for assault or obstruction as a consequence of this and, because of what appears to be an in-built prejudice, result in a high number of arrests of black people, especially young blacks. (IRR, 1979, p. 10)

The IRR argues that the SPG has changed its function from being a support anti-crime unit to a police command unit taking part in indiscriminate stop-and-search activities (and being used against pickets and at demonstrations). The IRR pointed out that, according to the statistics revealed by the Commissioner, 'extremely large numbers of people are stopped, questioned and searched by the SPG, with proportionately very few arrests as a result' (ibid., p. 10). They show that, in 1972, 41,980 persons were stopped and searched with 3,142 arrests; by 1976 the corresponding figures were 60,898 and 3,773 (in 1977 a figure for stops of pedestrians only was given as 14,018 with an arrest total of 2,990; in 1978 only arrests were given, 4,166, which may suggest a stops figure of well over 60,000). Commenting on these figures, *State Research Bulletin* stated that 'at the highest level, one in 10 (in 1973) were arrested and at the lowest, one in 16 (1976): why the remaining tens of thousands should have been stopped and searched for no good reason remains unexplained' (*State Research Bulletin*, 1979, p. 135).

Lambeth, in particular, has borne the brunt of the 'attacks' by the SPG. 'Swamp 81' was only the latest operation at the end of a long line of such operations in the area. Between 1975 and 1979 there were six such 'attacks' by the SPG on the people of Lambeth. Each time the pattern was similar – road blocks, early-morning raids and random street checks (Working Party on Community/Police Relations in Lambeth, 1981, p. 6). Of the '18,907 stop and searches by the SPG in Greater London in 1975 some *14,000* took place in Lambeth and Lewisham during a two month period – resulting in just 403 arrests. Of the 5,000-odd stop and searches in the rest of the Metropolitan area, some 3,700 resulted in arrests' (*Time Out*, 17–23 April 1981, p. 12). The

Commander of the local police force ('L' District) since 1976, Len Adams, was formerly SPG Commander and the operational controller at the Red Lion Square demonstration (ibid., p. 12). In 1978 'over half the total strength of the SPG, 120 officers, supplemented by 30 extra officers from Scotland Yard were drafted into the Lambeth police area because of its alleged "high crime rate". Over 1,000 people were stopped on the streets and 430 people arrested; 40% of those arrested were black, more than double the estimated black proportion of the local community. The SPG operation was concentrated around four housing estates, all with high black populations' (Working Party on Community/Police Relations in Lambeth, 1981, p. 6). The police reply is that these methods are essential to general crime prevention and especially useful to combat 'crime waves' (particularly in 'muggings'), or in the area of a serious offence, or during periods of terrorist activity. However, it would be interesting to know more on the ethnic background of those stopped and searched, also of those taken temporarily into custody and then released without charge. What does seem clear is that abuses in the use of 'sus' and the arbitrary use of stop-and-search would seem to be complementary forms of harassment often used against black people. Finally, the IRR may be wrong in saying that the SPG has changed in function from an anti-crime to a police command unit. The recent activities of this 'mobile reserve' could be seen as the inevitable outcome of its original remit, as 'swamping' an area for stop-and-search purposes (at least in the MPD) may be more of a quantitative than a qualitative development. The police, however, still deny that these squads are a specially selected, trained and equipped riot force or in any way 'para-military' (Commissioner of Police of the Metropolis, 1977, p. 27).

The debate on 'sus' became a focus for the wider discussion of police powers and practice as many of the issues it involves raise questions in relation to civil rights and criminal procedure. The Home Office, the Director of Public Prosecutions, the Magistrates Association, the Association of Chief Police Officers, the Police Federation and the Police Superintendents' Association are asking for important changes in criminal procedure to make prosecution easier and for large extensions in police powers. To a great extent they have followed the lead set by Sir David McNee in his evidence to the Royal Commission on Criminal Procedure (RCCP) where he pressed for increased powers for the police to stop, search, and arrest, the abolition of the right to silence and the present caution, and the extension of detention for up to seventy-two hours without charge.

It is rather ironic, and particularly unfortunate, that the terms of reference considered by the Royal Commission were largely set, in practice, by the police in their uncompromising requests for less legal and other restrictions on their work. The massive pressure by police organisations to restrict the already meagre rights of the defendant provided by the Judges' Rules is the result of the belief that anomalies in police powers and certain administrative restrictions on their work lead to an 'unfair' advantage on the part of the defendant up to and including the trial. Yet, the Royal Commission, it is generally agreed, was finally set up following the disturbing revelations given by the Fisher Report on the Confait case, although the need for an examination of legal procedure was expressed before the *Report*'s findings (RCCP, 1981, p. 3; Fisher, 1977). Among the other revelations of this very disquieting report was the serious malpractice in the way in which the police had gained statements and confessions and the general disregard (even by senior police officers) of the Judges' Rules and Administrative Directions (that is, the 'right' to communicate with relatives and a solicitor). It is important, for both the community and the police, that these 'rights' be safeguarded. The Community Relations Commission, in evidence to the Select Committee on Race Relations and Immigration (1971/2), emphasised the importance of the Judges' Rules stating that 'much of immigrants' mistrust could be traced to what happened or was thought to happen at police stations' (IRR, 1979, p. 45). It is noticeable that those organisations (and others) who have called for the abolition of 'sus' have also generally advocated that the Judges' Rules should be given legal backing.

By seeking to dismantle the existing protection given to the defendant (covering interrogations, the taking of a statement and access to legal representation) the police 'lobby', the Home Office and the DPP are pressing the debate in the opposite direction to safeguards for civil rights. They are attempting to re-draw the boundary between citizens' rights and police authority. The danger of any such inevitable boundary, no matter where it has to be drawn, is that the police will tend, in practice, to overstep it if not restrained or deterred, to ensure a successful prosecution. The likely result is, rather than the conviction of the 'experienced criminal', an injustice done to the innocent and vulnerable. The opposing argument, put by Sir David McNee treading in the path of Sir Robert Mark, is that because the 'guilty' are being acquitted the police feel frustrated because they are denied the reward of conviction for their efforts. Outdated legal hindrances in their powers produces, he admits in an astonishing statement, short-cuts in police practice: 'Many police officers have, early in their careers, learned to use methods bordering on trickery or stealth in their investigations because they were deprived of proper powers by the legislature' (Commissioner of Police of the Metropolis, 1978, p. 2). One inference which can be drawn from this confession is that the Metropolitan Commissioner is wishing for the legitimation of routine abuses or 'manipulations of the law', a view perhaps confirmed in a speech he gave on the same subject: 'All the necessary powers to deal effectively with criminal behaviour must be clearly within the law. Otherwise the law itself is brought into disrepute' (*Guardian*, 19 June 1979).

The *Report* of the Royal Commission on Criminal Procedure was published on 8 January 1981 (RCCP, 1981). The legal establishment generally welcomed the report and saw it as a very important contribution to the necessary reform of criminal procedure. Even so, there was disquiet expressed regarding the safeguards laid down for the suspect's rights. Edward Du Cann, QC, Chairperson of the Bar Council, expressed some concern about the new power of arrest being proposed and questioned whether the sanctions against police who breach the rules outlined would be effective. Press reaction was also rather mixed. Again, there was a general welcome but disquiet was also expressed by some newspapers about the safeguards being proposed for the suspect. *The Times*, for instance, accepted a number of the report's recommendations but also pointed to its central weakness, 'on the whole, the Commission has succeeded in drawing that fine balance on paper' between police powers and suspect's rights 'but its recommendations require that society place a level of confidence in police behaviour, and in their commitment to the laws and rules laid down, that cannot be taken for granted' (*The Times*, editorial, 9 January 1981). Not surprisingly, the police have warmly welcomed the report, although certain of its recommendations (for example, the proposal for a separate local prosecution system) are not favoured by them. While they have not said as much about the report as might have been expected (perhaps trying to judge the intent of the Home Office and government), Jim Jardine and the Police Federation have given the report their blessing. The Police Federation in its magazine under the subheading 'Nice one Cyril' noted that its own recommendations had not been met in full, but nevertheless the 'Commission's views come close to Federation evidence' (*Police*, 1981, p. 15).

'Sus' receives only a very brief mention in the Royal Commission's *Report*. It notes that there had been 'considerable controversy' surrounding the offence both before and during the Commission's inquiry and comments that a 'substantial amount of evidence on the matter' had been received. The report concludes that the Commission

> were deeply concerned about the friction between certain sections of the community and some police forces which the use of the provision undoubtedly causes, but the offence itself, being part of the substantive criminal law, is, strictly speaking, outside our terms of reference. Our consideration of the matter has, however, been overtaken by events. The subject has been examined by the Home Affairs Sub-Committee of the House of Commons on Race Relations and Immigration. We welcome the government's announcement of its intention of bringing forward legislation which will include the repeal of the suspected person offence [In the Queen's Speech, November 1980] and we hope that this will contribute to the improvement of relations between the police and young people, particularly those in minority groups. (RCCP, *Report*, 1981, pp. 49–50)

Despite at first seeming to rule out its ability to make a recommendation, a recommendation is, in fact, being made. Support is not given to the total abolition of the offence, as argued for by many of the groups giving evidence to the Royal Commission and by the Home Affairs Sub-Committee, but to the government's policy of replacement and, implicitly to the main contents of the Bill which had been made fairly clear by various statements made by William Whitelaw.

It is generally agreed that the Royal Commission has recommended an extension of police powers of stop and search, arrest, detention, and 'sample' taking. The report called for a statutory code of practice to replace the Judges' Rules; road blocks to be permissible if there were reasonable grounds that a serious offender was in the area or a serious offence might take place; stop-and-search powers would be brought under one power applying to stopping a person in the street, and search where there was 'reasonable suspicion' that stolen goods or prohibited items were being carried; renewable detention of suspects; the fingerprinting of 10-year-olds; the arrest without warrant on 'reasonable suspicion' of committing an offence carrying a penalty of five years or more; the rejection of the automatic exclusion rule (except where evidence is obtained through torture or unhuman or degrading treatment) on evidence which has been illegally or improperly obtained. These are only some of the far-reaching recommendations and it is not possible to discuss them in depth. However, some discussion of the report's attempt to 'balance' these greater police powers with increased safeguards for the public (including closer supervision by superior officers of the work of lower ranks) is required. First, the 'balance' the Royal Commission has tried to strike rests on the initial acceptance of the general case for extra police powers rather than merely making existing powers more consistent (which may have produced some specific extensions). Dissent was expressed by Jack Jones and Wilfred Wood, the Barbados-born canon of Southwark Cathedral, who pointed to the implications of many of the recommendations, including the likely effect on police–community relations, that greater police powers would bring. Many of the important proposals are offered without the support of any evidence and in spite of the facts provided by its own research. Secondly, time and again the Commission says it has been guided by the principles of 'fairness', and similar terms, and claims its proposals are 'workable'. Rules were being laid down which provided for constant review and sanctions for their breach which were 'close to the event'. However, if we read beneath the various statements of high principle and intent, it becomes clear that with the extensions of police powers that the report contains and the weakness of the safeguards – which remain internal and provide for numerous exceptions – some of the often-stated fundamental principles of our criminal justice system are under threat.

Two examples are sufficient to show the nature of this threat – the proposals on interrogation and stop and search. It is a fundamental principle that statements should be voluntary (even though we know the frequency of police abuse, more recent prominent examples being the stolen 'dinky toys' case, and the evidence by witnesses at the Deptford fire inquest). Yet, the Commission argues in a rather tortured logic that because the very fact of being in a police station is intimidatory, in a similar way, pressures by the police cannot be controlled. They are all part of the facts of the situation. Thus 'uncontrollability' is used, in a perverted fashion, to justify police misconduct. In practical terms, 'the proposal would mean that statements and confessions which have been induced by prolonged interrogation, sleep deprivation, ill-treatment short of torture, a promise of bail' or threats to charge relatives will be admitted in evidence. 'Magistrates and juries would be merely advised of the danger of acting upon such statements' (McConville and Baldwin, 1981, pp. 179–80). The proposals for stop and search are also dangerous since they further undermine the principle that there should be protection from random searches and from searches based upon mere generalised suspicion. The Commission makes the broad statement that those who have in their 'possession' articles which it is a criminal offence to possess should not be entirely protected from the possibility of being searched' but, as McConville and Baldwin argue, this begs the question of what is an offensive weapon (car tools, steel comb, penknife?) and opens the way for random searches. In fact, the Commission seems to uphold the idea of general and discriminatory searches 'Where a gang of youths turns up at a seaside town on a Bank Holiday', or 'football supporters are on their way to a match', or 'where the police, from experience, believe that criminal offences are likely to result from a group's activities, because, for example, one or more of them may be carrying offensive weapons'. Here, the Commission's 'safeguard' of 'reasonable suspicion' flies out of the window and the police are left with the freedom to operate (against young blacks and others) according to prejudice (see McConville and Baldwin, 1981, p. 179).

The Legal Action Group (LAG), the NCCL, the Haldane Society of Socialist Lawyers and other bodies have already voiced strong criticisms against the proposals by the Royal Commission (see *Legal Action Group*, February 1981). Community, welfare and race groups still need to make their opposition clearer. An important event, in this respect, was the report prepared for Lambeth Council by a working party headed by David Turner-Samuels, QC (and including two Labour Councillors and one Conservative, and the CRC chairperson, after the breakdown of formal relations between the police and the black community. After taking into account nearly 300 submissions by individuals and organisations, the report concluded that an 'extremely grave' situation had come about through the lack of democratic control of the police and by the particular nature of police measures. It recommended that some changes could be made to bring some improvement in police–community relations: giving the Judges' Rules the force of law, no increase in police powers, and stopping the use of the SPG in the borough. In regard to the recommendations of the Royal Commission, it stated that the police already act as if they had the power to set up road blocks to stop all traffic, the power to stop and search people to prevent or detect serious crime, the power to seize property found in a public place that could be useful in evidence, and to obtain names and addresses of witnesses. Finally, the report called for the repeal of Section 4 of the Vagrancy Act 1824, for it not to be replaced 'in whole or in part' (Working Party of Community/Police Relations in Lambeth, 1981, pp. 85–8). Only a matter of weeks from the date the report was published the police again 'invaded' the area in the operation 'Swamp 81', but this time they were met, following a week of the campaign, by violent resistance.

It was very unfortunate that the members of the Commission who were presumably recruited to represent voices outside the law and order establishment (and hence give the final report greater legitimacy) were divided. Jack Jones and Canon Wood seem to have been a dissenting minority against some of the major extensions of police powers, but they did not write a minority report (although Jack Jones did publicly register his fears regarding the effects of the changes on community–police relations). However, Walter Merricks (former Director of Camden Law Centre) and Dianne Hayter (Secretary of the Fabian Society) have strongly defended the report (especially its 'safeguards') and have reacted rather bitterly to criticism from black groups, radical lawyers and the left (including the Labour Party). Their reaction was fully supported by the influential legal writer, Michael Zander who argued in the *Guardian* that Merricks and Hayter were firmly in the 'civil liberties corner' and would hardly sign a police charter (Zander, 1981b). His view was that the report represented 'a major step towards significantly better safeguards for the accused' and dismissed criticism as a 'left wing knee jerk reaction' – sentiments which not only were in marked contrast to *Guardian* editorial comment but (as LAG pointed out) placed him somewhat to the right of Richard Du Cann and the Bar Council (Zander, 1981a; *Legal Action Group Bulletin*, 1981, p. 33). Perhaps more surprising, is the initial acceptance, or lack of sufficient critical awareness of the nature of the 'safeguards' among some writers and academics, usually considered to be on the left, who could previously have been described as critics of police pro-cedures and practice (see, for example, Kettle, 1981). With a closer and more reflective reading of the report (and bearing in mind the implications on the ground of the proposed powers, past and present police practice and the ineffective basis of the 'paper' on 'theoretical' safeguards) the dangers in the report become obvious.

A forceful and united body of criticism (and counter-proposals, including the widening of the debate to encompass greater external accountability) of the report from all those welfare bodies, ethnic groups and civil liberties and political organisa-tions is urgently needed. There are signs, at last, that the Labour Party is no longer fully supporting the bi-partisan approach to law and order issues (shared with the Conservatives) and that there is a growing recognition, even amongst the leadership, of its sorry record on civil liberties. Roy Hattersley, the Shadow Home Secretary, condemned the report's recommendations on the power to stop and search, the extension of the power to arrest without warrant, the power to hold a suspect in twenty-four-hour deten-tion without charge (as undermining *habeas corpus*), and the compulsory taking of fingerprints of suspected children aged between 10 and 13. He concluded that the changes will do 'little to quieten the fears that the practices often employed in the investigation of offences can result in a denial of rights and liberties that a free society should never withold from its citizens'. The effect of the measures would be to increase tension between the police and the community, especially ethnic minorities (*Guardian*, 13 January 1981).

In addition, the recent election of local Labour Councils committed to the greater accountability of the police to the community is another hopeful sign of a change on civil liberties issues within the Labour Party. However, the Labour Party has still a long way to go in formulating a new approach to 'law and order' and, of course, with the present government in power with three years to run the omens are not good for greater safeguards against police malpractice and liberal criminal justice reform. Indeed, the passage of the Criminal Justice Act (Scotland) and police demands for local measures curtailing the right to demonstrate, point in the opposite direction (Baldwin and Kinsey, 1980). The outcome of the Scarman Inquiry into the events surrounding the Brixton 'riot', the recommendations of the committee set up by William Whitelaw to inquire into changes in riot gear (following the very public lobby by the Association of Chief Police Officers, the Police Superintendents' Association, and the Police Federation), the results of police pressure to change the law on riot, after the failure of riot charges against the Bristol defendants, are eagerly, if apprehensively, awaited.

The Wider Significance of the 'Sus' Issue

The campaign against 'sus' and the police malpractices it revealed certainly played an important role in the abolition of the offence although it failed to prevent the introduction of the Bill making 'interfering with a motor vehicle, etc.' an offence. However, there are definite indications that, along with the new powers under the Criminal Attempts Bill, the massive stop-and-search operations, and possible new widespread powers as a result of the Royal Commission on Criminal Procedure, that the police are prepared to use new technical equipment to aid street control and surveillance (the new police helicopter is only the most visible example). The criticisms levelled against 'sus' charges may even have helped to spur on, if only marginally, this trend. Some indication of possible future developments can be gained from the example of the 'Islington 18' case in 1977 and its aftermath when the Metropolitan Police pressed mass conspiracy to rob charges. The exercise ended very disappointingly for the police as out of a possible ninety guilty verdicts only eight were given after a trial of three and a half months. The evidence of the police were found to be either suspect or contradictory (*Sunday Times*, 5 November 1978). The police were far more careful in their procedures in the 'Lewisham 21' case in 1978 in assembling their evidence of identification and in the treatment of suspects, so that any possible defence criticisms concerning false identification and forced confessions could be neutralised. Detective Inspector John Grieve, in charge of the operation, said in court, 'Before this began, I was left in no doubt as to what would happen to me if this trial displayed police incompetence and malpractice' (*Sunday Times*, 5 November 1978). A significant new feature of police methods was the use of video-film taken over three days and photographs by a team of ten who watched bus stops for six weeks. These were shown in court in the attempt to prove that the defendants were at bus stops trying to steal women's purses. Surprisingly, the film and photographs showed no actual offences taking place but the material was a major piece of evidence against the youths. Again, rather surprisingly in view of the intensive police surveillance, charges were not brought for any observed crime during the period such as 'sus', attempted theft, or theft from the person. Instead, the broad charge of conspiracy to rob was laid against 21 people on a list of 100 suspects (some of them white) that the police had compiled. The accused were given sentences of up to three years.

In the view of the police, those who criticise this action want the argument both ways; when they do present 'independent witnesses' – photographs and video-film – an abuse of civil liberties is alleged. But this switch to technological forms of observations, which may give the appearance of scientific impartiality in court, is, if anything, more controversial in terms of civil liberties than the specific charge of 'sus'. In addition, the use of conspiracy to rob charges raises again the whole issue of conspiracy charges which are notable for the difficulties of providing a defence due to the vague or non-specific nature of the charge, the presumption of guilt, and the acceptance of evidence which for other charges is inadmissible. With conspiracy charges, there is also the possibility of a penalty which is stiffer than that for the actual offence (if it had been committed). A further disturbing feature of police practice in the case was a dawn raid by 150 police officers on nearly thirty houses in Deptford to arrest the youths which is reminiscent of operations against terrorists and would seem inappropriate for the detention of young pickpockets.

The police have begun to enter into political debate much more openly by publicly advocating changes in the law which they insist are needed for efficient law enforcement. Instead of the traditionally accepted view of the relationship between the police and politicians and government (that is, Parliament consists of the democratically elected representatives of the community, who formulate laws which the police are responsible for carrying out), we have witnessed a rather different relationship emerging. The police have set the pace of legal debate by a crusade against what they see as restraints on their work and by demanding legal changes to strengthen 'law and order'. While the traditional or theoretical relationship was never quite so simple in practice, in recent years the giving of advice to policicians and the odd public speech or statement has turned into a full political campaign, over the heads of politicians, for public support. The writings and speeches of Sir Robert Mark, Sir David McNee's pre-emptive public-relations strike to gain support for his evidence to the Royal Commission on Criminal Procedure and set the boundaries of discussion, and the Police Federation's 'non-political' law and order campaign during the last election (continued during the last hanging debate and pursued in Parliament by its retained adviser Eldon Griffiths, MP) are the most visible examples of this campaign.

Any attempt to counter this campaign or re-set the terms of reference for the debate on police power must be careful not to ignore wider interpretations for the changes in policing and the emergence of a strong police ideology. The concentration on calls for greater police accountability, different training and education, however necessary, may overlook the explanation behind the trend towards authoritarianism and moral fundamentalism of the holy trinity of McNee, Anderton and Mark.

The changing social function of the police must be seen within the wider societal shifts and, particularly, state policy, that are taking place. The long-term social and economic problems of a nation in relative decline, in addition to the recent economic crisis, have raised social tensions and conflicts. The police become an important institution for the crisis management of a society in conflict as it is the first to meet, and be asked to cope with, the results of state policy through the imposition of order. It is this greater stress on the maintenance of order and social peace which has placed increased strain on the various, possibly contradictory, duties of the police – impartial law enforcement, protection of citizen's rights, and the establishment of social order. Finally, it must be remembered that the police are given the 'routine' duty of controlling an unequal society, therefore the call for more accountability is a necessary, but ultimately limited, demand.

The significance, for the police, of the charge of 'sus' is not only that it can be used as a general deterrent by clearing certain groups from areas of commerce and trade, but also that it has the advantage of providing an ease of conviction through the nature of the charge and evidence. To that extent it is a model for the powers which the police wish to have for the detection and prevention of other offences; the shift of the onus of proof on to the defendant to establish innocence, further restrictions on the right to trial by jury (and possible straight majority verdicts), and greater powers to stop and search, and arrest, are all features of the police campaign. Issues raised by this relatively minor offence (although it can carry a prison sentence of up to a year on second conviction) has wider implications for the future of law enforcement. It is because of the wide discretion, the easily assembled evidence, and the high conviction rate which characterises the offence, and the vulnerability of the police to criticism on their use of the charge which led them to a vigorous defence of Section 4 of the 1824 Vagrancy Act. If it was to be abolished, they argued, some effective measure would still be needed to fill the gap in the police preventative measures required for street policing. The strength of the police defence was due to the fact that if it can be demonstrated that increased powers create unacceptable abuses – as in the case of 'sus' – then clearly this evidence casts a very disturbing shadow over the police campaign for legal changes (and shows at least some community resistance to it) to shift the balance between citizens' rights and police powers. The Scrap Sus Campaign was very important, although it was not able to achieve the full abolition of 'sus' (without replacement), not simply because it brought to a wider public evidence of abuses by the police in procedure (including racial bias) and demonstrated the likely outcome of powers which give the police wider discretion and easy conviction, but also because it was an effective organisational response of local black communities to excessive police 'freedom' – a response which has stimulated campaigns against wider police practices (for example, SPG use, interrogation abuses, lack of defence against racialist attacks, etc.) and wider political issues.

I wish to thank Tony Jefferson for his comments on an earlier version of this chapter.

8 Social Policy and Black Youth

GEORGE FISHER and
HARRY JOSHUA

Black Youth as a Problem

As with so many other aspects of British domestic race relations, the emergence of 'black youth' as a discrete 'social category' has been a piecemeal, disjointed affair, clouded in competing ideologies and explanations, and steeped in crisis.

Demonstrably, the social factors and processes involved began to take shape in the late 1960s and early 1970s with the gradual realisation that not only was the education system failing the black second generation 'achievement-wise' (Plowden, 1967; Coard, 1971) but was also intrinsically incapable of delivering liberal formulations and visions of integration. In short, the other side of the educational mountain was not to be that 'promised land' in which, as Roy Jenkins said in 1966, 'equal opportunity ... would be ... accompanied by cultural diversity in an atmosphere of mutual tolerance'.

Whereas black underachievement in schools tended, in the short term, to stimulate issues largely restricted to the field of education (Rex and Tomlinson, 1979, p. 62), the same could not be said of the high and disproportionate incidence of unemployment amongst black school-leavers (Stevenson and Wallis, 1970; D. Smith, 1977). Coupled with official fears concerning 'alarming levels' of homelessness, particularly amongst West Indians (CRC, 1974, p. 10), the black second generation began to be singled out and identified as the central yardstick against which more general race relations and immigration policies had to be assessed. In the words of a contemporary Home Secretary: 'The *real* challenge of Race Relations still lies ahead of us as first generation immigrants bring up their children in our midst; our children, British children born in this country. This is the challenge which we shall reject at our peril' (Robert Carr, 11 October 1973, Blackpool).

On these foundations, throughout the 1970s the progressively hardening link between young blacks and criminality provided the central social imperative, reinforcing and elaborating the notion of black youth as a distinct social category amenable to both professional sociological study and to specific policy responses. Indicative of the manner in which this link was originated and extended, between 1972 and 1973, based on highly contentious statistical techniques, the official police stance on the issue of blacks and crime underwent a dramatic reversal. Blacks, formerly 'statistically invisible', were suddenly found to be over-represented 'in respect of every main category of crime' – or such at least was the conclusion drawn from arrest figures for the London area compiled by the Metropolitan Police (Select Committee, 1976–7, Vol. 1, p. 30).

Simultaneously, the emotive label 'mugging', a legally impre-cise media term for a whole range of petty street crimes, began to gain increasing credence in relation to the criminality of young blacks located in the multi-deprived, inner-city zone (Hall *et al.*, 1978). With the victim typified by the media as white and often helpless, for many social commentators, mugging heralded a new era of racially directed crime. Accordingly, relations between the black second generation and the relevant controlling agencies of the state deteriorated, as the courts responded with heavier exemplary sentences, and the police with rigorous enforcement of the 'sus' law. (For a detailed analysis, see Chapter 7.)

Against such a background, arguably it hardly needed the emotive prompting of the explosive 1976 Notting Hill Carnival to bring sharply into focus established patterns of social dis-advantages specific to black youth and, more important still, their whole cultural, ideological and political articulation within the 'host' society.

Reflecting the new urgency with which this particular aspect of race relations was officially regarded, the CRE chose to entitle its 1980 study on black youth, *The Fire Next Time*. Whether warning or prediction, the 'Fire' referred variously to 'the very real dangers . . .' and the 'crisis, which would have deeply felt and long lived repercussions throughout our cities . . .' should society fail to meet the challenge of 'alienated' black youth. This alienation – varying in intensity from those who were 'already virtually or totally alienated from society' to those who were simply 'at risk' – the CRE argued, was not necessarily permanent or irreversible. Though founded on job discrimination, inner city multi-deprivation, cultural and identity problems, family conflict, and black 'life-styles', those social agencies concerned with the pro-blem could yet build 'bridges' allowing alienated black youth to pass from being 'adrift from society' on the one side, to achieving a 'full and rewarding life' on the other. This diagnosis, we believe, speaks for itself. It needs only be added here that even the CRE – in discussion papers which preceeded *The Fire Next Time* – recognised another 'solution' to the 'challenge' of alienated black youth so formulated, i.e. firm control by those agencies of the state concerned with law and order.

Black Youth Analysed and Categorised

Of the political and policy implication posed by the above, more will be said later. For the moment, however, some explanation seems necessary of the various processes through which the sociology of race relations have come to invest the term 'black youth' with form and meaning.

In order that black youth might be sociologically, that is, 'scientifically' explained, first a recognisable social group had to be identified and isolated. This isolating/explanatory process, however, rather than an exercise in even conventional academic rationale and method, demonstrated from its very beginnings a greater empathy with the social formulations, concerns and designs of the body politic. In short, that body of sociological literature purporting to deal with black youth was not primarily informed by any overwhelming desire to document and order the myriad of situations and strategies applicable to the black second generation. Instead, by far the more discernible were the influences of successive crises posed by young blacks and the corresponding social and moral panic of the state; both instructed by the 'problem orientated' sociology associated with the first-generation colonial immigrant.

Initiating the isolating/explanatory process from which the social category 'black youth' was eventually derived, meant that young blacks had to be structurally differentiated from white youth. For Miles (1978, pp. 13–14), sections of black and white working-class youth, having been 'failed' by the education system, went on to share joint disadvantage in the employment market. Subject ultimately, however, to the distinctive 'history of slavery and colonialism' specific to West Indian youth, these similarities could not be taken too far – particularly regarding the different cultural responses to deprivation. More commonly, it was the observation that those social problems generated by black youth could not be explained in terms of 'juvenility' or 'adolescence' that provided the main justification for their isolation from white youth. Few significant implications for the analytical framework within which black youth was conceptualised appeared to follow. If white youth and its adolescent revolt could be accommodated within a schema of non-structural subcultures signified and experienced within a relatively auton-omous complex of folk heroes, distinctive modes of behaviour, speech, music and dress, then so also could black youth. If white youth could be socially contained by a system of state provision based upon a 'get 'em off the streets, constructive use of leisure time' philosophy (G. John, 1978, p. 15), then, with minor modifica-tions, so also could black youth. This descriptive rather than theoretical disjuncture with white youth apart, it was in relation to the black community in general that attempts by academics and officials to isolate black youth were most pronounced and determined; in some instances, formulated in terms of a 'complex' generation gap. In others, around those differential social charac-teristics intrinsic to the colonial immigrant population born abroad, as opposed to those born in Britain. Whatever the case, the end result has usually been the same – a structural schism between the first and succeeding generations, symbolised by conflict and distrust, but based upon their supposedly different and unrelated locations within dominant metropolitan society.

What, then, came to be the popular attributes of this genera-tional divide? According to the Select Committee on Race Rela-tions and Immigration 'young blacks' were:

> British born citizens who feel they have every right to be so recognised and have no wish to be designated West Indian. Indeed, the young blacks mark the emerging division in the adult West Indian commun-ity between the immigrant and the indigenous black: between the old generation with its West Indian background and tradition and the new generation brought up and educated in the United Kingdom.' (Select Committee, 1976–7, Vol. 1, pp. 25–6)

Troyna, by contrast, emphasised the passivity and misguided optimism of the first generation (Troyna, 1979). In the hands of Brake, however, the generational crisis assumes its full economic, cultural as well as psychological dimensions:

> The parents of black and brown youth were immigrants, and as such prepared to put up with difficulties here, helped as they were by a culture with its roots outside Britain. Their children are second and third generation immigrants, members of the previous host popula-tion, yet are still rejected by it. Immigrants, a self-selected group of ambitious people, are often sustained by the belief they will return home, even though this is a fantasy. For their children, the Indian sub-continent, Africa, the Caribbean are not places they have grown up in, and these become nostalgic fantasies, substitutes for the bleakness and racism of Britain. Young non-white Britons are British, but the rejection they suffer causes them to turn to reject the British, and the crisis of identity suffered is devastating. (Brake, 1980, pp. 115–16)

A full statement of the intergenerational problematic implicit in these and other representations would be beyond the scope of this chapter; its central features, however, may be summarised as follows:

If the original colonial immigrant population posed for the British state a number of social, sometimes race-relations problems, then to a substantial extent these could be explained in terms of 'strangeness', on the one hand, and 'culture', on the other. Deployed, however, in relation to specific immigrant groupings, or to their specific circumstances, these central conceptual tools invariably conjured up a confusing, if not contradictory, picture.

Whereas all colonial immigrants were deemed 'strangers', in the sense of not having 'achieved that easy familiarity with the host culture which enables them to compete on an equal footing' *The Times*, 23 May, 1976), they were also strange as a consequence of their 'alien' cultures. In the case of West Indians, where superficial similarities with English cultural forms, norms and values appeared to deny the notion of 'alien-ness', other suppositions – as, for example, Landes's (1955) vaguely biological invention the 'archetypal stranger' – could be substituted in its place. Whatever its origins, the social consequences of strangeness were expected to decline with time. Culture, however, presented a dual and contradictory problem. On one level, it permitted continued strangeness and isolation and thus was to be resisted. On another level, it could be allowed, even encouraged, as a central feature structuring the social organisation and attitudes of the first generation.

Within this 'explanatory framework', then, the first-generation colonial immigrant was made comparatively unproblematic. Therefore, it was not incidental that they were frequently characterised as 'law-abiding', 'hard-working' and 'uncomplaining'. If they were obliged to accept a subordinated position within the host community, then, generally speaking, this represented 'progress' compared with their former lot back home. In any event, their structural position could be accounted for largely in terms of the immigrant's own inability to adapt to the British way of life. Only in a secondary manner did such factors as racial prejudice and discrimination impinge. While issues relating to the role of the state, and the requirements and motives of capital in the 1950s and 1960s, were considered almost taboo.

By these means, not only could the first generation be detached from the second, but the former dispatched to the analytical periphery, retaining significance only in so far as they were perceived to transmit inadequacies and deprivations. The second generation, by contrast, born and educated in the UK and thus fully acculturated and no longer strange, had to be analysed differently. Compared with their parents the second generation of blacks had been socialised to expect the same opportunities as their white counterparts. In reality, their expectations have not been fulfilled (D. Smith, 1977). Consequently, they were represented as bearing the full brunt of racial prejudice and discrimination in addition to all the implications of inner-city multi-deprivation (CRE, 1980*b*). Detached from the cultural heritage of their parents – which, and whom, they came to reject – and unable to achieve social, educational and economic parity with their white peers, they became an 'alientated generation'. These, then, were the 'real' problems of race relations.

A major addition to the growing number of pathologies seen as afflicting the black community, intergenerational conflict has also similarly expanded the list of stock conventional explanations. No explanation of homelessness amongst young West Indians, for example, would be complete without some reference to the cultural inadequacy of the West Indian family: 'Often parents were said to have authoritarian or Victorian attitudes which were bound to clash sooner or later with the more liberal attitudes their children were absorbing from British Society' (CRC, 1974, p. 49). Nor could parental shortcomings be ignored in relation to either educational achievement or performance in the employment market:

> The parents who had themselves come to live in Britain without gaining any experience of going through the British Educational system were acknowledged to be in a difficult position in giving their children the support and encouragement that non-immigrant parents might be able to give. This meant, it is said, that particularly for West Indians, parental encouragement was sometimes lacking or (where present) of an unrealistic and over ambitious kind. The parents' limited knowledge of the details of qualifications required for particular occupations made the situation worse. (ibid., p. 31)

Dislocated from white youth, and placed in opposition to the first generation, it is through the inter-related concepts of alienation and subcultures that the final isolation and realisation of the social category 'black youth' is achieved.

Despite underlying similarities in the incorporation and subordination of Asian and West Indian immigrant labour, based almost entirely on contrasting cultural responses to migration and settlement, both immigrant communities were held to be differently located within British society. The nature of Asian cultural traditions required Asian youth to have no specific need for distinctive subcultures. Accordingly, it has been concluded that Asian youth were not 'involved in the same type of alienating processes as Caribbean youth' (Brake, 1980, p. 18).

The term 'black youth', then, was primarily intended for that special class of West Indian youngsters, usually in conflict with their parents' generation; 'often kicked out of their homes'; 'who do not register for work, who are aimless, rootless drifters concerned with "hustling" for a living' (C. Cross, 1978); 'cultural conflict', 'alienated' and 'adrift from society' and from the 'instruments of law and order' (CRE, 1980*d*). As a group they had partly evolved, and partly readopted Jamaican Rastafarian ideologies, symbols and practices, then constructing within the British environment a distinctive and compensating subculture.

With this primary and highly specific social category informing the sociology of the black second generation, the resulting tendency to characterise that group as problematical and threatening may be seen as most readily manifested in the growing number of social studies being currently produced on Rastafarians and the Rastafarian movement. Few of these studies, however, have managed to escape accusations of wholesale obfuscation and distortion (Campbell, 1980). Not only have they signally failed to penetrate and understand Rasta ideologies and practice, but in attempting to account for the development of Rastafarianism in Britain, have revealed an underlying incoherence confirming a number of important limitations and inadequacies intrinsic to the isolating/explanatory methodology commonly employed. For instance, having virtually equated Rasta 'subculture' with the social category 'black youth', and having comprehensively isolated black youth from its parent generation, culture and homeland, it is to that same homeland that researchers have returned in order to explain metropolitan variants of Rastafarian ideological and cultural modes. Having posed for black youth an identity crisis originating in a dual culture clash with parental and metropolitan cultures, the same black youths are then portrayed as positively involved in both re-articulating and extending radical, though increasingly central, aspects of the indigenous home culture. Having dispatched Rastafarianism to the realms of an autonomous, or semi-autonomous, youth subculture, the ideological element within that subculture is explained with reference to the forms and lyrics of reggae, a musical idiom generated primarily with the home environment, and enjoyed throughout the West Indian population in Britain.

Clearly, the cultural/ideological disposition of the black West Indian second generation cannot be conceptualised in terms of subculture and explained independently of the complex and changing racially imprinted class position of colonial immigrant labour. In that colonial immigrant labour is increasingly marginalised within contemporary British metropolitan society, the key questions posed relate to the manner and mechanisms through which this process disproportionately affects the black second generation. Nor in this context can either the colonial or historical dimensions be ignored. Over and above the need for a thoroughgoing periodisation (hopefully ending once and for all that popular tendency to link aspects of West Indian culture directly to slavery), the proposition that the colonial experience of the labour process is being essentially, though differently, reproduced with regard to black youth in Britain begs serious examination. Rather than a social category isolating those elements most threatening to the state, the contention here is that the black second generation cannot be explained except in relation to those structures subordinating their parents born before and after immigration.

Race and Social Policy

Policy-makers and 'problem definers' were loathe to abandon the early policy perspectives and goals formulated in respect of the first-generation immigration and race relations. Secondly, a basic hegemony had been established with elements of the first-generation black population which the state was anxious to reinforce rather than dismantle. Lastly, and probably crucially, given the series of crises through which the black second generation had come to impose themselves on the national political consciousness, the whole debate concerning the specific nature of the provisions necessary tended to follow in the wake of more immediate and direct responses by those controlling agencies of the state concerned with the maintenance of law and order.

In relation to the manner in which those policies specific to black youth came to be formulated, undoubtedly influential were the definitions, perspectives and goals previously determined in the period of primary immigration up until the late 1960s. Indicative of the issues central to this period, few aspects of the race-relations debate could not be related back to the question of numbers. Black immigrants were seen as posing a threat to British cultural life. They were 'taking away jobs' from the white working class; they 'put a strain on the social services'; they presented schools with 'enormous problems', and so on. In the name of 'harmonious race relations,' therefore, the black 'invasion' had to be controlled, if not stopped. Without such controls, immigrant areas, often regarded as ghettos, would continue to expand in the inner zones of many larger British cities – an aspect seen as antithetic to any successful strategy of integration. Prior to the mid-1960s, in so far as such a strategy existed it was concerned primarily to provide a 'welfare service' through local volunteer committees. Gradually, as these groups became more formalised and interconnected, the National Council for Commonwealth Immigrants (NCCI) was established (Abbot, 1971). This body eventually received government recognition and funding in 1965.

In accordance, however, with the dominant socio-political outlook of the day, both the NCCI and its successor in 1968, the Community Relations Commission (CRC) defined their activities around the promotion of 'racial harmony' – the assimilation of the colonial immigrant stranger. Two important strands emerged in seeking to obtain 'harmonious community relations' – the legal as distinct from the social. Racial prejudice and discrimination in terms of the law became the responsibility of the Race Relations Board (RRB), whilst the CRC became preoccupied with public relations and education. The attempts to treat race relations from this dual standpoint caused confusion and frustration. In order to minimise the confused situation the Commission for Racial Equality (CRE) was constituted to replace the CRC and the RRB.

Immigrant numbers and 'concentrations', on the one hand, and a welfare approach to immigrant problems, on the other, constituted the central conceptual elements informing initial race-relations policies. Within this overall perspective, political expediency further demanded that policy issues could not be made race specific. This much was clearly stressed in the 1965 White Paper outlining the terms of reference for the CRC: 'It should be emphasised at every stage that this is not a committee to serve the interests of any one section of the community, but a committee to promote racial harmony. It is therefore beneficial to all.'

According to the same White Paper, community relations was to be based on: 'Voluntary immigrant and host community participation, local authority involvement and a non-sectarian and non-political stance.' That this formulation drew little sustained opposition from immigrant organisations demonstrated the extent to which they had already come to accept official definitions and prescriptions with regard to race-relations problems. Over and above the lure of additional status, synonymous with official involvement, the island-based supportive and recreational constitutions of many early West Indian immigrant organisations (Pearson, 1977) did not in any essential manner

contradict the basic philosophy of official policy on race. Whereas
the same could not be said about more politically oriented black
protest organisations, when traditional parliamentary lobbying
tactics were employed, for example by the Campaign Against
Racial Discrimination (CARD), they proved to be only marginally
effective in opposing the official immigration policies of the 1960s
(Heinemann, 1972).

By the mid-1960s, a network of official and unofficial structures
existed purporting to deal with problems of race relations. It had
been constructed around the state's miserly estimation of the
needs of first-generation immigrants, and with the agreement
and active participation of sections of the immigrant population.
In so far as questions relating to the emergence of black youths
were concerned, most government officials and immigrant leaders believed that they would be easily settled within British
society. After all, second-generation blacks would be 'fully acculturated' and 'adjusted' to the complex metropolitan environment.
They would be 'educated in Great Britain', and thus would be able
'to take full advantage of all the opportunities' not available to
the first-generation immigrant. Except for the provision of special classes and English as a second language, necessary to
ensure that children of new arrivals were successfully assimi-
lated into the educational system, young blacks could either be
ignored or dealt with within the same policy framework applicable to their parents.

Consequently, for the Department of Education and Science in
the mid-1960s, what was described as a 'potentially serious
situation' with regard to Indian children in Southall referred
primarily to the issue of concentration and dispersal. In DES
circular 7/65 (1965) arguments were reported of protesting white
parents who considered that the presence of immigrant children
in the schools was having an adverse effect on their own children's education. The then Minister of Education, now Lord
Boyle, suggested a limit of 30 per cent in any one school. DES
circular 7/65 recommended that, wherever possible, schools
should keep to the 30 per cent limit; this could be achieved by
re-marking catchment areas, or by physically dispersing immigrant pupils. The circular reasoned that:

> Apart from unusual difficulties (such as a high proportion of non-
> English speakers) up to a fifth of immigrant children in any group fit
> in with reasonable ease, but as the proportion goes over about one
> third in any one class, serious strains arise. It is therefore desirable
> that the catchment areas of schools should wherever possible be
> arranged to avoid undue concentrations of immigrant children. When
> this proves impracticable simply because the school serves an area

which is occupied largely by immigrants, every effort should be made to disperse the immigrant children around a greater number of schools .... It will be helpful if the parent of non-immigrant children can see that practical measures have been taken to deal with the problem in the schools, and that the progress of their own children is not being restricted by the undue preoccupation of the teaching staff with the linguistic and other difficulties of immigrant children.... It is to everyone's disadvantage if the problems within the schools are allowed to become so great that they cause a decline in the general standard of education provided.

The question of in whose interests these measures were seen as necessary, hardly needs to be asked.

Britain had already undergone fundamental change. In short, that range of social problems specific to, and informing, the primary social category 'black youth' had either already emerged, or were in the process of emerging. The consequences of this were of significance in two important respects. First, with under-achievement in schools (Giles, 1977), poor employment oppor-tunities, intermittent and long-term unemployment (Lewisham CRC, 1978; Dex, 1978–9; CRE, 1980b) and homelessness (CRC, 1974) now endemic to a growing section of the black population, that section began to throw up numerous militant black organ-isations sympathetic to radical black nationalist, and even revo-lutionary, ideologies. Secondly, in that these problems tended to manifest themselves in petty street crime, they pre-empted a massive police intervention in black neighbourhoods, backed up with a law and order campaign directed at black youth (Jeffer-son *et al.* 1975; Hall *et al.*, 1978). Few could doubt the over-whelming impact of this latter feature in defining the character of race relations throughout most of the last decade, particularly in the light of the 1976 and 1977 Notting Hill Carnivals, events at Brick Lane, Southall and Bristol. Further, that this was allowed to be the case, comments directly not only on the inadequacies of official policies, but also on the lack of the state's political will, even ability, to evolve and administer constructive solutions.

Refusing to discard many of the central propositions shaping the formulation of policies in the period of primary immigration, changes in governmental attitudes noticeable in the early 1970s represented little more than a rehash of old solutions in a new guise. Officially, racism and the race specific could still not be publicly conceded with regard to policy categories and structures for fear of alienating the silent white majority. Thus, in defining race-relations problems, the immigrant assimilationist perspec-tive (that is, language problems and insufficient knowledge of

British society) was still thought to be highly relevant, but in conjunction with inner-city deprivation, namely those problems that immigrants 'shared with the indigenous community but which are even more serious or on a proportionately larger scale, for example, difficulties in getting the best out of the school system and differences in family structures which require differential responses from the social services' (Home Office, 1978). The logic in the 1977 White Paper *Policy for the Inner City* (DoE, 1977) suggests that if resources were to be allocated to tackle problems of multi-deprivation in the inner urban areas, the ethnic minorities resident therein would be amongst those who stood to benefit. Additionally, the well-tried welfare approach was also to be continued though, in this instance, administered through acceptable elements amongst those very same militant black organisations in the form of 'Self Help Schemes'.

In 1974, therefore, the Home Office made a grant of some £250,000 to the then CRC (later, in 1976, the Commission for Racial Equality) for the purposes of assisting black self-help groups. The rationale of this self-help programme was to allow 'victims of discrimination and disadvantage to come to grips with their problems' (CRE, 1978a). Conceding the growing centrality of black youth, the programme's objective was to: 'support existing self help projects and to encourage new ones, primarily, but not exclusively, for the benefit of young West Indians who were homeless and/or unemployed and who were considered to be beyond the reach of the normal social services' (ibid.). Later, however, the Asian community was also admitted to the scheme.

Notwithstanding the very real effect this self-help strategy has had in diffusing the militancy and integrity of once-autonomous radical black protest organisations and in facilitating a sense of dependency within the wider black community, on the level of addressing the problems of black youth the results of this programme to date have been little more than marginal. Indicative of the relationship the CRE developed with its clientele, there has been an appallingly low record of take-up and severe underexpenditure. Out of a budget of £500,000 in 1978–9, the actual sum spent was £140,000. Out of 150 applications received under the scheme between 1974 and 1978, only 25 projects received funding. In explanation, the CRE blamed the immigrant groups, on the one hand, and the Home Office, on the other.

It is clear, however, that 'black' projects (self-help or otherwise) are closely related to official resources. In view of this, black self-help schemes follow a particular course in their development. Any deviation leads to inevitable conflict between the 'black projectors' and the officials.

In the main, all black projects accommodate one, or a few, of the following areas in their task of dealing with 'problems':

(1) Supplementary schooling/education.
(2) Social life-skills courses.
(3) Job creation.
(4) Accommodation/hostels.
(5) Youth clubs.
(6) Information/advice.
(7) Detached workers.

This pattern of development is largely determined by official guidelines. The social welfare basis of the self-help schemes dates back to the early 1960s, and still hinges upon the 'stranger' hypothesis of that period in particular programmes, for example, social and life skills and information/advice. The major difference being that, in the main, the 'contact' workers are increasingly black themselves. This latter development has prompted Gus John to speak in terms of a 'black social service', a trend that is closely linked to the 'black youth' phenomenon, with all the attendant pathologies. (Black workers in this context may be, therefore, regarded as 'cooling towers' with specific tasks to perform.)

Another conception of black workers in Social Centres which was popular in the late 1970s was to see them as surrogate parents. By adopting this view, the prescription for the alienated black youth and all the problems they faced is parental understanding and presumably a stable family relationship. Moreover, this conception of alienated black youth suggests that they are 'stray' from the 'socialising influences' of 'established institutions'. So the task for black workers must be to bring them back to these institutions. (A 'black social' service may have its attractions in terms of ethnic identification, etc., but it is not likely to improve the material conditions and secure equality of black people in society.) Ironically, black workers have neither the resources nor the 'clout' to make any meaningful impact on the appalling material conditions facing young blacks. They cannot offer them jobs, housing, and access to education and training. They have negligible influence on the institutions and organisations which practise discrimination and perpetuate racism.

Within this framework, black workers, at best, can only hope to minimise black youth–police contact by 'keeping them off the streets' or at least by postponing conflict. Self-help projects are short-term and, in many cases, 'one-offs'; increasingly, black youths are becoming independent and are outgrowing the 'project scene', thus they 'hang out' elsewhere – in cafés, record shops and the bookies.

In the absence of meaningful changes in their circumstances and environment, young blacks will continue to evolve 'coping strategies' and strategies of resistance in order to survive in society. The law and order lobby will of necessity respond, resulting in a spiralling police and black youth conflict.

Perhaps the time has come to reappraise the whole race-relations field and to abandon the old colonial ideals for more realistic practices. Surely the old welfare approach of the 1950s and 1960s must have outlived its usefulness? The law and order campaign of the 1970s has not worked so far, instead the effect has been to sharpen hostilities between the police and the black community as a whole, for example, the response by black leaders' call for 'no co-operation' with the police at their conference held in June 1980 (*Guardian*, 30 June 1980).

It is interesting to note that immediately following the Bristol disturbances in April 1980, Merlyn Rees, Shadow Home Secretary, reported on BBC Radio 4, that the SPG's should be set up 'in these areas' – he meant the inner-city immigrant areas.

The extent of the frustrations in British domestic race relations has been made explicit in the CRE Report 1980*b*, when the chairman openly pledged support for a black civil-rights movement. At the same time, black organisations all over the country rallied around the call for an alternative, broadly based civil-rights movement.

Clearly, such a movement has a contribution to make and in that it has already firmly distanced itself from the race-relations establishment, it has made an early impression on the black community. Ultimately, however, its success in bringing pressure to bear on the state, will depend upon its ability to mobilise wide ranging and mass support throughout both the immigrant and host communities. Whereas this is likely to be anything but painstaking, long-term and probably reformist, those social problems confronting the black second generation are urgent and require considerably more than the mere, unwilling legal intervention of the state.

9 Confusing Categories and Neglecting Contradictions

SHEILA ALLEN

There are those who act with great confidence in matters relating to young black people.

The Recorder at the Inner London Crown Court in pronouncing sentences of six years' imprisonment on four black youths (aged 18–19) said:

> These were serious offences and you were in possession of weapons to bring guerrilla warfare into the streets of Lewisham. If only one of these milk bottles had been thrown and exploded the consequences could have been very serious. It would have caused panic in the crowd and injuries and an immediate riot and destruction of property. The courts must take action to prevent conduct of this nature and it is my duty to impose severe sentences to deter others.

A lawyer, condemned the sentences as 'sadistic, barbarous and savage.' He said the courts had a duty to balance in equal measure those who provoked violence as against those who were provoked. 'This sentence will be seen in the black communities as the courts of law siding with the National Front and against the black communities', he claimed (quoted in the *Guardian*, 22 October 1980).

During the same week, a 27-year-old Birmingham-born woman (young and black) is reported to have been refused permission after a four-year fight to have her three children, aged between 6 and 9 years, to live with her and her husband in Britain (*Morning Star*, 27 October 1980). Those taking this decision are less visible, as Home Office adjudicators, than the judge or the lawyer, but none the less decisive.

The cases quoted have their unique, individual attributes, but they are by no means unique or individual in the contemporary world of Britain. An understanding of cases such as these rests on an analysis of the ways in which social relations are structured, and part of this relates to the ways in which the intellectual endeavour has itself been structured. Policy evaluations or propositions about policy initiatives are based by professional social scientists on their claim to intellectual clarity about the social construction of sets of social relations and the issues or problems to which these give rise.

The category 'black youth' is a construction which either facilitates or hinders the analysis. I shall argue that such a category oversimplifies the structure of a class society and the relations of culture within it which function to reproduce the social relations between classes, generations, genders and ethnic groups.

Scholars of race relations have been engaged for a quarter of a century or more in Britain in attempts to come to terms with the problems created by disciplines firmly based on Eurocentric and ethnocentric assumptions. The context in which the disciplines were located was influenced by the migration of those from colonies and ex-colonies, who came to work and to live in Britain during the 1950s and 1960s. The migration was relatively small, though this is not obvious from some of the descriptive terms used by social scientists. The social and political response was, however, significant and was influenced both by local concerns and political events and changes beyond the shores of Britain.

The world of professional social scientists was penetrated by some aspects of these changes but it would be mistaken to overstate the impact on the social sciences. There was nothing akin to the ramifications experienced by institutional social science in the USA. There has been no attack, concentrated or otherwise, by black scholars on the white intellectual hegemony; in part, because such scholars in Britain can be numbered if not on one hand, then on two.

The source of the impact in Britain was largely from white liberal social scientists who were aware of the comparative material and the historical dimensions of the problems as well as of the intellectual developments elsewhere, particularly in the USA. They were concerned to inject these dimensions into the intellectual discourse and to affect the policy-making process. Much of the early work was reactive scholarship, pursued in response to the definitions of the problems produced by politicians, social workers, education authorities, central and local government departments, and the media. In the public sphere these definitions consistently adopted a parochial perspective and commonly associated the causes of the problems with the immigrants thus disadvantaging the already disadvantaged. Immigrant youth was no exception to this pattern.

As a long-standing critic of the work based on a migrant–host framework and on the 'stranger hypothesis', I see such attempts within the context of a weakly developed social science in Britain as far as the dimensions of race and ethnicity were concerned. They nevertheless echoed, in some respects, aspects of the writings of black authors, such as James Baldwin, who wrote of the 'simplicity of [a] European village where white men still have the luxury of looking on me as a stranger'. He explained this as follows, 'Europe's black possessions remained – and do remain – Europe's colonies, at which remove they represented no threat whatever to European identity. If they posed any problems at all for the European conscience, it was a problem which remained comfortingly abstract; in effect the black man, *as a man*, did not exist for Europe' (1965, p. 149 and pp. 144–5).

An evaluation of the context in which the work of an earlier generation of social scientists was set needs to be made. There were always those willing to produce research which supports the dominant ideologies, and the pervasive integrationist ideology of the 1950s and early 1960s found such support, and still does, though the main body of such work was, and is, on the fringe of social science. It was never the approach, for instance, of Kenneth Little, Michael Banton or John Rex. It was explicitly criticised in the work of the succeeding generation of Stuart Bentley, Michael Lyon, Robert Moore, and many others.

With the advent of separatist approaches, borrowed largely from the USA, but pursued in Britain in a political context of increasingly overt institutional racism (including the undeniable, though frequently denied, racism of governments of both dominant political persuasions), came an intellectual challenge of considerable proportions. It produced, on the one hand, those who regarded separatist approaches simply as ideological manifestations of black racism and who dismissed their relevance or validity to the social, scientific and political context. At the other extreme, there were those who became what Genovese (1971) characterised as 'House Honkeys'.

The challenge, both in the intellectual and political contexts, of separatist approaches dates back to the late 1960s in Britain, and is still being worked through (Oral History and Black History, 1980). It posed a range of complex problems, the core of which is to be found in the separate socio-cultural realities of the black experience. The current discussion of black youth must be set, at least in part, within this context.

An equally important development was a shift in emphasis which was initially quite separate from and pre-dated, in Britain, the emergence of black separatist ideas. The struggle to define the 'dark strangers' as workers enmeshed in an international economic system was largely ineffectual until the burgeoning interest in the dependence of European economies on *Gast-arbeiter* became influential (see Allen, 1970). The body of literature on this during the early 1970s invaded British parochialism and made explicit a variety of questions which had been studiously ignored by many concerned with British race relations (Castles and Kosack, 1973). One debate which emerged more forcibly than before was the inter-relation of race and class and its specificities in the British situation. It is not my intention to follow the history of this debate but to note its continuing relevance to the subject of this book. Recognition needs also to be given to the slowly developing awareness of the complexities introduced into the discussions by, for instance, Teodor Shanin's insistence that the pre-migration experience should not be obliterated from metropolitan class analyses. He summarised very cogently the issues which were conveniently neglected in the early 1970s (Shanin, 1978).

A critical reappraisal of the inter-relation of black experience, peasant and urban migrations and the socio-economic conditions underlying class formation is therefore necessary to an analysis of young, black people in Britain.

The lack of research-based evidence of the lives of the generation who came in the 1950s and 1960s creates problems for analyses of young black people in the 1980s. Some of the comparisons being made between the older generation and the younger one appear to be based on very thin evidence and border dangerously on the stereotypes created by official commentators, social scientists, social workers, teachers, and the like. Generalisations that the earlier generation were 'quiescent', 'prepared to accept their lot', 'willingly did the lowly paid, low status work', 'had low expectations for themselves' need much closer examination. It can be argued that such a characterisation denies the level of awareness that the older generation had of the conditions of their existence. It denies, too, their experience of colonial oppression and the part some of them had played in attempting to combat and change the circumstances of their lives. Some of those from the Indian subcontinent had been engaged in the independence struggles themselves, and many had come from areas and families which had a long history of such struggle. Experience in the armed forces in the Second World War of many of the men cannot be discounted in the formation of their views, or the assessment of their situation, when they became immigrant workers in Britain. Furthermore, it is important not to assume that an acute appreciation of the constraints and obstacles confronting them is equivalent to 'quiescence' or 'acceptance'.

To make invisible much of the experience of these generations in order to sharpen comparisons with the attitudes and behaviour of their young adult sons, leaves a number of problems unresolved and creates several new ones. When analysing the contemporary situation we have to acknowledge that many questions remain open and to close them by stereotypical portrayals of the older generation is a denial of generational experience and produces an impoverished analysis.

It is not only the question of the separate socio-cultural realities of black and white members of society which need careful exploration. We must look, too, at the modes of analysis which have emerged in social science theories about generational relations and, in particular, in the research on youth.

The sociology of youth and the psychology of adolescence are two broad areas in which questions were posed and which have informed much of the work on specific problems. The problems were defined most commonly by practitioners or authority figures and the responses of social scientists were related, in large measure, to these.

In the 1950s and early 1960s the main sociological framework of analysis was provided by those, Eisenstadt (1956), for instance, who used a normative functionalist approach based on the model of Talcott Parsons. The adjustment of youth to the major value orientations and symbols of a particular society was considered the core of the problem. The processes of socialisations, therefore, became central to the explanation (see Allen, 1968, 1973). Variations of the Parsonian model of socialisation are still highly influential.

Socialisation depends to a large degree on the theories of developmental psychology – the socialisation of the person into the role. Developmental psychology takes for granted most of the issues which have concerned critical theorists and produces a mechanistic, a historical, a situational account of complex processes situated in circumstances it does not examine. Its use of the concept of role is uncritical, despite the theoretical shortcomings pointed out by, among others, Margaret Coulson (1972). Role theory constrains without facilitating our understanding of what happens between parents and their children, within institutions and peer groups. And it neglects the wider contexts of economic and political circumstances in which these parents, children and peers live.

One body of work relating in some respects to generational relations, within minority groups, adopts some aspects of this approach but without the explicitness found in the Parsonian framework. Dissatisfaction with the earlier integrationist models gave way to pluralist analyses. Most commonly arising as an acknowledgement of cultural diversity among Asian minorities and between them and the majority groups, cultural pluralism was put forward as a description and as an explanation. Work on young people of Asian descent was set within a framework of the cultural conflict of being between 'two' cultures. What is perhaps most interesting about this development in the context of this chapter is that, on the whole, it is confined to Asians and only rarely used for Caribbean groups and that culture refers to 'home' cultures – religion, dress, language, marriage patterns, food, and so on – and is either vague about the majority culture, or refers not to culture but to the 'social demands of the wider society' (Watson, 1977). The work using the two cultures, cultural pluralism approach, appears to be carried on uninfluenced by the subcultural approach developed in the 1970s (see Anwar, 1976).

Much of the work produced in the late 1960s and early 1970s arose from dissatisfaction with the limitations of the Parsonian framework and was part of a rediscovery and revision of Marxist approaches. The passive, adaptive view of socialisation with its mechanistic underpinnings was challenged and perspectives adopted which emphasised creative interaction, and stressed relevance and meaning rather than external constraint. The widespread activities of students which challenged authority structures led to propositions about the radical or revolutionary potentialities of student movements. Such propositions fitted the view that the intelligentsia, not the working class, was the potential agent of revolutionary change, but the onus was placed on the young (Rowntree and Rowntree, 1968; Nairn, 1968). The arguments need not concern us here, except to note that there are similarities between the vocabularies used to describe the students, their dress, language and activities, and those currently adopted in some discussions of black youth.

The other area which emerged related, in the main, to working-class youth and much attention was focused on the phenomenon of the Teddy Boys, mods and rockers, and skinheads. The accounts were centred on styles of dress, language, music and leisure activities connected with sport, predominantly football and motor-cycles. Assessments related these unsympathetically to the first affluent generation freed from the disciplines of hunger, humiliation and the dole queues. Sympathetically, they were related to resistance and deviance and the moral panics of authority characteristic of divisions between generations.

It was recognised that youth was not classless and that relations between generations did not take place in a structural vacuum (Murdock and McCron, 1976). The concentration was on elements within working-class youth (increasingly labelled sub-cultures) and predominantly on deviant youth.

Hebidge recognises this tendency when he states:

> Though it is important to distinguish between the delinquent gang (small, with a specific local recruitment, a local set of loyalties, and a strong commitment to 'machismo', subterranean values and illegal activities) and the sub-culture which is altogether broader, looser, less strictly defined by class and regional membership and less literally involved in law-breaking, there are obvious connections (e.g. gangs like the Quinton Boys, a group of Midlands skinheads, can exist within sub-cultures). Moreover, the two terms are virtually synonomous in the popular mythology. Unfortunately, the confusion that follows from this association (about class, violence, etc.) has all too often been reproduced in academic work because the analysis of sub-culture grew in large part directly out of the study of delinquent street gangs. (1979, pp. 180–1)

Relatively little attention was given to working life or family life, or the inter-relations of these with leisure, and the stress was almost totally male in terms of the researchers and the researched. The descriptive accounts, obtained in some instances by participant observation, relied heavily on culture or subculture as an organising, ordering concept. The ambiguities which attend this concept were largely ignored. It could be argued that the ambiguity has been compounded by the adoption of a model drawn largely from a deviancy approach and applied uncritically to many, if not all, manifestations of 'youth cultures'.

In relation to youth, the most thorough-going attempt to situate culture and subculture within an overall framework is that of Hall and his colleagues. Like Mungham and Pearson (1976), they argue that the concept of youth culture and most of the empirical work on youth neglected the structure of class relations. They describe a dominant–subordinate culture and discuss the necessity of locating subculture as an element of the 'parent' culture. They locate youth subcultures at the 'inter-section between the located parent culture and the mediating institutions of the dominant culture' (Hall and Jefferson, 1976, p. 53). They see generational differences (they stress the many elements common to different generations) in terms of the adaptation, negotiation and resistance borrowed from the parent culture and adapted by the young for its distinct 'focal concerns'. The idea of distinctive generational location and experience is underpinned in their argument by evidence of postwar changes of both the material and ideological environment.

Their insistence that youth has to be located in the central structures and dynamics of society constitutes an important advance on the literature of the 1950s. However, the gap between the theory and the ethnography of subcultures remains disturbingly wide. The ethnography is almost exclusively concerned with 'deviant' categories, strongly reminiscent of the delinquent gangs. It is a leisure-oriented, street, café and disco 'culture' dependent for its recognition on 'style'. Life-style (that is culture) (Hall and Jefferson, 1976, p. 123) reveals an intellectual position narrowed to suit this perspective.

> Working class sub-cultures ... take shape on the level of the social and cultural class relations of the subordinate classes. In themselves they, too, win space for the young: cultural space in the neighbourhood and institutions, real time for leisure and recreation, actual room on the street or street corner. They serve to mark out and appropriate 'territory' in the localities. They focus around key occasions of social interaction: the weekend, the disco, the bank-holiday trip, the night out in the centre, the 'standing-about-doing nothing' of the weekday evening, the Saturday match. They cluster around particular locations. They develop specific rhythms of interchange, structured relations between members: younger to older, experienced to novice, stylish to square. They explore 'focal concerns' central to the inner life of the group: things always 'done' or 'never done', a set of social rituals which underpin their collective identity and define them as a 'group' instead of a mere collection of individuals. They adopt and adapt material objects – goods and possessions, and reorganise them into distinctive 'styles' which express the collectivity of their being-as-a-group. These concerns, activities, relationships, materials become embodied in rituals of relationship and occasion and movement. Sometimes, the world is marked out, linguistically by names or an argot which classifies the social world exterior to them in terms meaningful only within their group perspective, and maintains its boundaries. This also helps them to develop, ahead of immediate activities a perspective on the immediate future – plans, projects, things to do to fill out time, exploits ... They too are concrete, identifiable social formations constructed as a collective response to the material and situated experience of their class. (Hall and Jefferson, 1976, pp. 45–7)

The mediating institutions of the dominant culture are, typically, the commercial youth-culture market, the police and agencies of legal control, and the media as reproducers of the control culture, and the socialisers are the informal agencies – the family and neighbourhood.

The conceptual picture is painted with a broad brush which is fitted uneasily on to the ethnographic accounts and there is a failure to explain the criteria for selecting the 'groups' studied.

It is as though the culture of the adult working class were

related through studies of working-class clubs or pigeon fanciers to the neglect of the culture of work, the culture of collective attempts to alter working conditions, the practice of trade unionism, or the processes of political and economic incorporation and the resistance to it.

The exception in the ethnographic work on youth subcultures is the 'most common and intense activity engaged in by the majority' and 'the largest and most complex youth sub-culture' described by Corrigan (1976). His description of the majority as 'doing nothing' leads to a serious questioning of the claims that studies of deviant subcultures provide a basis for a more general understanding of the lives of the young. Moreover, Corrigan's findings tie in well with those of a national study which reports that 'watching T.V.' is the activity most commonly followed by 16-year-olds (Fogelman, 1976).

The concept of culture, as adopted within dominant sociological approaches, with its shared cultural norms of a classless structure and the mechanistic processes of socialisation into these norms, has been criticised as being limited because it does not add anything to the endeavour to understand culture as a dynamic and creative activity of human beings (see Bauman, 1973, p. 158 and pp. 169–70). Much of the youth subculture research could fit into such a limited concept, but where it is claimed for a concept of culture that it does provide for such an understanding, then the more general ambiguities of the concept cannot be set aside. If working-class youth subcultures constitute a break with dominant sociological analyses they would, nevertheless, appear to have incorporated elements of both the hierarchical and differentiated concepts of culture. The dominant–subordinate idea is heirarchical, both in ideological and material terms. The dominant controls, the subordinate responds, most creatively by resistance, but in the case of youth subcultures by 'imaginary solutions'. The generational subcultures (the range of those to be included is left unspecified except in the ethnographic detail) are differentiated from the parent culture, which in the case of the working class is a subordinated culture. The subcultures are explained in terms of 'expressing the reality and aspirations of the group' (Teds) 'expressing different meanings and sub-cultural values' (mods) 'symbolically re-creating parent culture' (skinheads) or in terms of 'its nature and effectiveness in life' (hippies/drug subculture).

If we accept, despite the continued ambiguities, that the subcultural theme has been followed because it appears to offer some lead into an understanding of creativity, activity, resistance, then it is difficult not to accept Bauman's view that

'Creativity boils down to the sheer expediency, cleverness and dexterity which guileful human beings display to turn an inhospitable environment to their advantage' (1973, p. 170). But since the creativity and resistance aspects of subcultures are characterised in an even more limited sense, 'There is no "subcultural solution" to working-class youth unemployment, educational disadvantage, compulsory miseducation, dead-end jobs, the routinisation and specialisation of labour, low pay and the loss of skills ... They "solve" but in an imaginary way problems which at the concrete material level remain unresolved' (Hall and Jefferson, 1976, pp. 47–8), we need to ask why they have been given such prominence at the expense of either the social activities of the 'non-deviants' or, perhaps more pertinently, of the struggles of young people at a concrete material level.

The methods of investigation pose the problems of the limits of the framework in a different way. The heavy reliance on interaction perspectives and transactional analyses has produced accounts insufficiently related to the parent culture and its structural subordination. To leave 'telling it how it is' or 'how it is experienced' as synchronic, restricted experiential accounts is to fail to confront the questions of specific structural locations, of dominated ideological forms and the encapsulation of contradictions in the socio-historical formations of which cultural histories are a part. From the multiplicity of experienced realities we can infer nothing if we assume that all reports of experience are equally valid. Positivist social science may have imposed a misguided or distorted order on these realities, but in rejecting a positivist approach we are still left with the problem of their ordering. Culture or subculture as presently developed do not appear to be very useful ordering concepts.

Butters tackles the problem from the stance of a critical review of participant observation (the most commonly advocated method) and he concludes

> what is at stake ... is not a universal "logic" of sociological enquiry, but the specific logics of the different techniques by which critical cultural studies can lay hold on the connections between different types of element in the socio-historical formation, and the articulation through which it achieves its complexly structural determinancy. (Quoted in Hall and Jefferson, 1976, p. 170)

The development of critical cultural studies and the problems associated with such studies are an important area in the study of black youth because of the attention given to the elements of style associated with reggae and the attempts to situate Rastafarianism within this kind of framework.

I want to turn to the statement I made initially about black youth and discuss some guidelines for research.

It is clear that I agree with those who argue that class location is crucial, and that, within this, generational similarities and differences must be mapped. To do this adequately the cultural history of both the working class and of the bourgeoisie, and their inter-relations not only of dominance and subordination but of struggle, material and ideological, are indispensable. The penetration, within Britain, of ideologies relating to blackness, to imperial domination and subordination and to ethnic ordering, into the structuring of class relations is part of this cultural history. Much of this is still ignored by historians and, in consequence, such locations are difficult to make, but to acknowledge the gaps is an advance on accepting historical myths (heroic or otherwise).

Additionally, however, the research on non-delinquent, non-deviant youth is mainly concerned with the 'problems' of the transition from school to work or the failure to achieve within the school system (see Brannen, 1975). Willis's account of working-class youth is a study of incorporation into the dominated culture of labour and remains an important exception (1977).

How do we interpret the findings of high levels of unemployment among young black urban males? A phenomenon pre-dating by at least a decade the present critical unemployment situation in Britain and a feature prominent in the USA for much longer (Stevenson and Wallis, 1970). Some of the earlier interpretations put the onus of explanations on the individual characteristics of black youths, usually referred to as 'immigrant' youth – the lack of educational achievement, of appropriate skills, language deficiencies, and so on; or, in another slightly different version, the youths were characterised as having unrealistic aspirations. Other work located the explanation in class terms, the structure of employment opportunity for working-class males and in the processes of everyday racism which disadvantaged black people (including young ones) in the labour market (Allen and Smith, 1975).

Some interpretations based on studies of subcultural style use the term 'rejection' or a synonym to characterise the behaviour of those who express rejection of 'slave labour'. This interpretation assumes that a choice to work exists which can be rejected. In a situation of full employment it may make sense to put forward such an interpretation. It can be argued that the poorly paid jobs with inferior working conditions, 'the slave labour' typically available in the 1960s, were rejected, though this claim has to be balanced by the evidence of the large numbers of young black people (and white) who took such jobs. In a situation of less than full employment (the situation of the 1970s) the system operated to select and reject, and colour was one criterion of selection and rejection. Expressions of rejection may be one of a few limited alternative responses which function as a strategy of personal or peer-group survival, developed in a hostile environment. Any specific response has to be analysed within the broader social context.

Where expressions of this kind are linked with 'an organising ideological framework' it can be hypothesised that they operate more effectively. It has been suggested, for instance, by Troyna and Cashmore (Chapter 5) that in the case of Rastafarianism 'massive changes in social consciousness' may be indicated. Put within a socio-historical context it may indicate a rear-guard action created by defeat in an oppressively racist structure. Unless the development of contemporary Rastafarianism in Britain is linked to the structures of domination and exploitation, and related to the lives of black people more generally, the changes in social consciousness and its implications remain questions.

Olivia Foster-Carter has argued that those who classify 'from the inside' using categories of lifestyles, are simplifying the realities of the lives of the black minorities into two polar oppositions and a mediating category, and are thus reinforcing negative stereotypes within the black groups and between the black minority and the white majority (forthcoming).

It underwrites the consciousness of black people more generally, 'in reality as colour is a significant symbol of classification no one can ignore it regardless of status, strategy or orientation. Therefore "mainstreamers" will be as conscious of their identity as any other category or sub-category.' And, furthermore, by defining some categories as a threat or as the sole political force, or as those with real leadership potential or as a social problem, she argues that there is a danger that such categorisation 'may become a rationalisation for the aggression of the majority'.

It is certainly the case that some of the categories used are those of the outsider and can, with little effort, be translated into the stereotypes of the dominant culture. The richness of the ethnographic data may be considered sufficient reason for the research. If, however, the aim is to 'make sense' of the data, questions arise about categorisation. The dangers and limitations of specific categorisation can be pointed up, as Olivia Foster-Carter does, using a structuralist analysis based on the work of Leach, Levi-Strauss and Douglas to provide a clearer understanding of the functions of categories and their relation to 'myths'.

Nevertheless, categorisations, despite any specific faults, are attempts to order cognitively our own or others' reality. This brings us again to the significance of clarifying what is meant by those who concentrate their research on 'sub-cultural styles expressive of meanings' or categorise on the basis of style. Without less ambiguity about the status of culture as an analytical tool, subculture only serves to mystify what it seeks to understand.

The more general problem, however, is that the perspective adopted directs attention (and research resources) away from the concerns with the majority and the structuring of their experience.

It is now a sociological cliché to state that the theory, methods and ethnographic material 'neglected', 'could not find', 'cannot incorporate' or simply 'forgot' the gender element. It is obvious, however, that it is by examining such 'gaps' and 'distortions' and their indications of how research resources are deployed, that the weaknesses of research on youth may best be summarised and guidelines for research developed.

Whatever the shortcomings of the interpretations of black unemployment, the portrayal of it as a male phenomenon ignores the official rates of unemployed black women. In addition, unemployment among young women from Indian, Pakistani or Bangladeshi families goes unrecognised because it is commonly assumed that 'cultural' constraints have operated to keep them off the labour market. They were thus doubly invisible (see Allen, 1980). Research on responses to unemployment would be greatly improved by the inclusion of young women's experience.

In terms of youth culture, even the 'new' approaches, such as those of Mungham and Pearson (1976), deplore 'our inability ... to recruit someone to write on the life of the working class girl'. Hall *et al.* (1978) include one chapter and a methodological note. This book also includes one paper (McRobbie and Garber, 1976). The male emphasis in subcultural studies renders young women marginal because, although the data on young women are generally scarce, what does exist indicates some gender differences are patterned early in relation to the use of space outside the home.

Much of the youth culture offerings of the postwar generation, McRobbie and Garber argue, can be translated by girls into 'the culture of the bedroom'; making-up, listening to records, chatting with girlfriends, dancing and reading 'teenage' magazines, and discussing boys. Such activities demand the appropriation of space. It has been estimated that something over a half of teenagers had 'private' space of a bedroom. Earlier studies had shown the home-centredness of girls, their stress on family relationships, the aspirations within the family and the lack of serious generational conflict. The keeping close to the family was both physical and symbolic in terms of the values expressed. The data on ethnic minorities, though even more scanty, indicates a similar constellation of lack of physical separation and lack of widely divergent evaluations between girls and their parents (see Delamont, 1980, ch. 4).

If girls do not go out so often, if they are expected to undertake housework and child care earlier and permitted 'a bedroom culture', if they earn less than their male peers, 'tip up' what they earn, portray a downwardly spiralling educational performance, and experience a heavily segregated labour market, then it is clear that the concerns of male youth culture will exclude them whether they are black or white.

We can hypothesise about differential patterns of social control by the dominant institutions (including the family), but our hypotheses must include the possibility that gender and class, rather than ethnicity, provide the structure of divisions so that the subordinated culture of the working class encompasses a clearly subordinated culture of the female gender. Even this kind of hypothesis raises questions about the discrepancy between the values expressed and the actual practices. For example, some on-going research indicates that for adult women the expressed values of gender relations are more non-traditional among middle-class couples, but that, in practice, their confinement to the wife–mother situation is greater than for working-class women (personal communication with Audrey Middleton).

Here we can find similarities with ethnic 'cultures' which stress confinement and control of women but, in practice, the women work outside the home and in doing so operate in contravention of norms. In the literature the norms are set out by middle-class professionals and reiterated by working-class respondents with the economic necessity of going out to work being given as a temporary extreme measure and accepted as long as the women collude in the dominant (male) explanation. The patterns of economic activity of women vary between regions, for instance, women's activity rates are higher in the south-east than in the West Midlands, even when religion is held constant. This must be explicable in terms of labour market opportunities rather than 'cultural norms' (Allen, 1980).

The 'affluence' of youth which is an underlying assumption of work on youth culture can only be understood if it is related to the social relations within families. Given that the earnings of most working-class young people, even before the present high level of unemployment, were limited, it is likely that parents subsidised their material existence. 'It seems likely that married women devote a higher proportion of their earnings to household expenditure, especially to expenditure for the children, than do married men' (Pahl, 1980). Given that we know so little of the flows of income between people within households, as Pahl shows, then we can know little of the control of material existence and values it expresses in the lives of different generations. The question of who pays for 'style' is one that has not so far been given much attention.

For an older age-group one style is described by Pryce and its material base is revealed:

> Whatever else the hustle might be, judged from the reference position of the dominant society, it is certainly not a deprivation. It restores the hustler's sense of pride and his feeling of mastery and autonomy.... [he] can live like a king and move about 'cool' and clean and well-dressed without any visible means of support ... The hustle is the ideal alternative to legal work because it is the complete antithesis.

Poncing is the favourite hustle.

> Poncing is ideal because it is the very antithesis of slave-labour, fulfilling all the hustler's wishes. (1979, p. 68, p. 75, p. 76).

Manhood is lost in 'slave-labour', it is regained at the expense of the subordination of women. These women are described as victims but also as capable of fighting back through manipulative techniques developed within the confined physical and social space available to them. They are always left to rear their children within worlds of physical and social violence.

How are such experiences to be located within the dominant institutions and the generational subcultures? The categorisation offered by Pryce is a comfortable, readily accepted version of how it is among the disreputable marginalised blacks of 'shanty-town'. It leaves unresolved and unasked questions of the physical violence aspect of gender relations which is not confined to class, ethnic or generational subcultures, but cuts across all of them. Consequently, it cannot be conceptualised as marginal; it has a clear material base in the ordering of the sex-segregated labour market and a clear ideological base in the normal social control institutions of marriage and child-rearing tasks.

What would be of interest is the development of cultural studies or cultural history which articulated the complexities of the everyday experience of both genders with the structures of domination and exploitation. The political problems underlying such efforts relate to the politics of liberation from gender subordination and class exploitation. The experience of young black women needs to be made visible, as does that of their mothers, so that the structuring of racism, as it affects them as well as their brothers, can be part of our understanding of 'black youth'.

The Contributors

ERNEST CASHMORE is Research Fellow of the Department of Sociology and Social History, University of Aston in Birmingham. His other books are *Rastaman: The Rastafarian Movement in England* (Allen & Unwin) and *Black Sportsmen* (Routledge & Kegan Paul). His next book will be *An Approach to Social Theory* (Heinemann Educational Books) written with B. Mullan.

BARRY TROYNA is Research Associate on the Education and Ethnicity Programme at the Research Unit on Ethnic Relations, University of Aston in Birmingham. He is on the editorial boards of *Multiracial Education* (the journal of NAME) and *Multi-Racial Social Work*. His book *Public Awareness and the Media: A Study of Reporting on Race* was published by the Commission for Racial Equality in 1981. His recent work on the National Front is published in *Race in Britain: Continuity and Change*, ed. Charles Husband (Hutchinson). He is also co-editor of *Race, School and the Labour Market* (National Youth Bureau). His next collaborative book with Ernest Cashmore will be *Introduction to Race Relations* (Routledge & Kegan Paul).

SHEILA ALLEN is Professor of Sociology in the School of Studies in Social Analysis, University of Bradford.

MALCOLM CROSS is Senior Research Fellow of the Research Unit on Ethnic Relations, University of Aston in Birmingham.

GEORGE FISHER is Lecturer in Education at Bayere University, Kane, Nigeria.

MARY FULLER is Senior Lecturer in Sociology at Bulmershe College of Higher Education, Reading.

HARRY JOSHUA is Research Associate at the Research Unit on Ethnic Relations, University of Aston in Birmingham.

JOHN REX is Professor of Sociology and Director of the Research Unit on Ethnic Relations, University of Aston in Birmingham.

BRIAN ROBERTS is a Lecturer in Sociology at North East London Polytechnic.

Bibliography

Abbot, Simon (ed.) (1971), *The Prevention of Racial Discrimination in England* (London: Oxford University Press for the Institute of Race Relations).

Acker, S. (1980), *Feminist Perspectives and British Sociology of Education*, paper presented at BSA annual conference (Lancaster).

Afro-Caribbean Education Resource Project (ACER) (1977), *Annual Report* (London: ACER).

Allen, Sheila (1968), 'Some theoretical problems in the study of youth', *Sociological Review*, vol. 16, no. 3 (November).

Allen, Sheila (1970), 'Immigrants or workers', in S. Zubaida (ed.), *Race and Racialism* (London: Tavistock).

Allen, Sheila (1971), 'Race and the economy: some aspects of the position of non-indigenous labour', *Race*, vol. 13, no. 2 (October).

Allen, Sheila (1972), 'Plural society and conflict', *New Community*, vol. 1, no. 5 (Autumn).

Allen, Sheila (1973), 'Class, culture and generation', *Sociological Review*, vol. 21, no. 3 (November).

Allen, Sheila (1980), 'Perhaps a seventh person?', *Women's Studies International Quarterly*, vol. 3.

Allen, Sheila and Smith, Christopher (1975), 'Minority group experience of the transition from education to work', in P. Brannen (ed.), *Entering the World of Work: Some Sociological Perspectives* (London: Department of Employment, HMSO).

Alderson, J. (1979), *Policing Freedom* (London: Macdonald & Evans).

Anderton, John (1979), 'A city and the finger of suspicion', *Guardian*, 6 January.

Anwar, Muhammad (1976), *Between Two Cultures. A Study of Relationships between Generations in the Asian Community in Britain* (London: Community Relations Commission).

Ascoli, D. (1979), *The Queen's Peace* (London: Hamish Hamilton).

Atkinson, P., Rees, T., Shone, D. and Williamson, H. (1980), 'Social and life skills: the latest case of compensatory education?', unpublished paper, University of Wales.

Bagley, Christopher (1979), 'A comparative perspective on the education of black children in England', *Comparative Education*, vol. 15, no. 1.

Bagley, Christopher and Verma, Gajendra (eds) (1979), *Race, Education and Identity* (London: Heinemann).

Baldwin, James (1965), *Notes of a Native Son* (London: Corgi).

Baldwin, R. and Kinsey, R. (1980), 'Behind the politics of police powers', *British Journal of Law and Society*, vol. 7, no. 2.

Barnes, Richard (1979), *Mods* (London: Eel Pie).

Barrett, Leonard (1977), *The Rastafarians* (London: Heinemann).

Bauman, Zygmunt (1973), *Culture as Praxis* (London: Routledge & Kegan Paul).

Bell, Daniel (1977), *The Culture Contradictions of Capitalism* (London: Heinemann).

Berger, Peter (1969), *The Social Reality of Religion* (London: Faber).

Berger, Peter and Luckmann, Thomas (1972), *The Social Construction of Reality* (Harmondsworth: Penguin).

Bernstein, Basil (1961), 'Social class and linguistic development', in A. H. Halsey, J. Floud and C. Arnold Anderson (eds), *Education, Economy and Society* (Glencoe, Ill.: The Free Press).

Birmingham Community Relations Council (1980), 'Analysis of inner city partnership grant aid, 1980', unpublished paper, August.

Bohning, W. (1972), *The Migration of Workers in the United Kingdom and the European Community* (London: Oxford University Press).

Bourne, J. and Sivanandan, A. (1980), 'Cheerleaders and ombudsmen: the sociology of race relations in Britain', *Race and Class*, vol. 21, no. 4 (Spring).

Boyd, D. A. C. (1978), 'Out of work', *New Society*, 25 May.

Brake, Mike (1980), *The Sociology of Youth Culture and Youth Sub-Cultures* (London: Routledge & Kegan Paul).

Brannen, Peter (ed.) (1975), *Entering the World of Work: Some Sociological Perspectives* (London: Department of Employment, HMSO).

Brent, L. and Crawford, J. (1979), 'Suspicious over "sus" figures', *Guardian*, 6 March.

Brown, John (1977), *Shades of Grey* (Cranfield, Beds.: Cranfield Institute of Technology).

Brown, W. (1980), 'We come from another field', in M. Prescod-Roberts and N. Steele (eds), *Black Women: Bringing It All Back Home* (Bristol: Falling Wall Press).

Bunyan, Tony (1977), *The Political Police in Britain* (London: Quartet).

Burney, Elizabeth (1967), *Housing on Trial* (London: Oxford University Press for the Institute of Race Relations).

Cain, Maureen (1973), *Society and the Policeman's Role* (London: Routledge & Kegan Paul).

Cairns, J. A. R. (1923), *The Sidelights of London* (London: Hutchinson).

Calley, Malcolm J. C. (1965), *God's People: West Indian Pentecostal Sects in England* (London: Oxford University Press).

Campbell, Horace (1980), 'Rastafarianism – the culture of resistance', *Race and Class*, vol. 22, no. 1, (Summer).

Carby, K. and Thakur, M. (1977), *No Problems Here?* (London: Institute of Personnel Management and Commission for Racial Equality).

Cashmore, Ernest (1977), 'The rastaman cometh', *New Society*, (25 August).

Cashmore, Ernest (1978), 'The social organisation of Canadian immigration law', *Canadian Journal of Sociology*, vol. 3, no. 4.

Cashmore, Ernest (1979a), *Rastaman* (London: Allen & Unwin).

Cashmore, Ernest (1979b), 'More than a version: a study of reality creation', *British Journal of Sociology*, vol. 30, no. 3 (September). Reprinted in P. Schulten (ed.), *Religious Movements* (The Hague: Nijhoff, 1981).

Cashmore, Ernest (1981*a*), 'The black British sporting life', *New Society*, vol. 57, no. 977.

Cashmore, Ernest (1981*b*), 'After the rastas', *New Community*, vol. 9, no. 2 (Autumn).

Cashmore, Ernest (1982) *Black Sportsmen* (London: Routledge & Kegan Paul).

Cashmore, Ernest and Troyna, Barry (1981), 'Just for white boys?', *Multiracial Education*, vol. 10, no. 1.

Castles, S. and Kosack, G. (1973), *Immigrant Workers and Class Structure in Western Europe* (London: Oxford University Press).

Cawson, P. (1977), 'Black children in approved schools', unpublished paper, DHSS.

Chambliss, W. J. (1964), 'A sociological analysis of the law of vagrancy', *Social Problems*, vol. 12 (Summer).

Clarke, Edith (1966), *My Mother Who Fathered Me* (London: Allen & Unwin).

Clarricoates, K. (1980), "The Importance of Being Ernest ... Emma ... Tom ... Jane." The perception and categorisation of conformity and deviation in primary schools', in R. Deem (ed.), *Schooling for Women's Work* (London: Routledge & Kegan Paul).

Coard, Bernard (1971), *How the West Indian Child Is Made Educationally Sub-Normal in the British School System* (London: New Beacon Books).

Cohen, Stanley (1973), *Folk Devils and Moral Panics* (London: Macgibbon & Kee).

Cohen, Stanley (1980), 'Symbols of trouble', in Stanley Cohen, *Folk Devils and Moral Panics* (London: Martin Robertson).

Coleman, J. (1961), *The Adolescent Society* (Glencoe, Ill. The Free Press).

Commission for Racial Equality (CRE) (1978*a*), *Looking for Work*, (London: CRE).

Commission for Racial Equality (CRE) (1978*b*), 'The Commission's role in self-help', unpublished document (London CRE).

Commission for Racial Equality (CRE) (1980*a*), *Ethnic Minority Youth Unemployment* (London: CRE).

Commission for Racial Equality (CRE) (1980*b*), *Half a Chance. A Report on Job Discrimination against Young Blacks in Nottingham*, (London: CRE).

Commission for Racial Equality (CRE) (1980*c*), *Youth in Multi-Racial Society: The Urgent Need for New Policies* (London: CRE).

Commission for Racial Equality (CRE) (1980*d*), *The Fire Next-Time*, (London: CRE).

The Commissioner of Police of the Metropolis (1977), *Annual Report 1977*, Cmnd 7328 (London: HMSO).

The Commissioner of Police of the Metropolis (1978), *Written Evidence to the Royal Commission on Criminal Procedure*, Part 1 (London: New Scotland Yard).

Community Relations Commission (CRC) (1974), *Unemployment and Homelessness* (London: CRC).

Corrigan, Paul (1976), 'Doing nothing', in S. Hall and T. Jefferson (eds), *Resistance through Rituals* (London: Hutchinson).

Coulson, M. (1972), 'Role: a redundant concept in sociology?', in J. A. Jackson (ed.), *Role* (London: Cambridge University Press).

The Cranfield Papers (1979), *The Proceedings of the 1978 Cranfield Conference on the Prevention of Crime in Europe* (London: Peel Press).

Cronon, David (1974), *Black Moses: The Study of Marcus Garvey and the Universal Negro Improvement Association* (Madison, Wis. University of Wisconsin Press).

Cross, Crispin (1978), 'Ethnic minorities and the labour market: the basic facts of disadvantage', in M. Day and D. Marsland (eds), *Black Kids, White Kids, What Hope?* (Leicester: National Youth Bureau).

Cross, Malcolm and Johnson, M. (1980), 'Migration, settlement and inner city policy: the British case', unpublished paper presented to the European Science Foundation Conference on Immigrant Workers in Metropolitan Cities, Birmingham.

Daniel, W. W. (1968), *Racial Discrimination in England* (Harmondsworth: Penguin).

Deem, Rosemary (ed.) (1980), *Schooling for Women's Work* (London: Routledge & Kegan Paul).

Delamont, Sara (1980), *The Sociology of Women* (London: Allen & Unwin).

Demuth, Clare (1978), *'Sus': A Report on the Vagrancy Act 1824* (London: Runnymede Trust).

Department of Education and Science (DES) (1965), *The Education of Immigrants*, DES circular 7/65 (London: HMSO).

Department of Education and Science (DES) (1978), *Special Educational Needs* (The Warnock Report), Cmnd 7212 (London: HMSO).

Department of Employment (DE) (1980), 'Racial discrimination at work', *Department of Employment Gazette*, vol. 88, no. 10.

Department of the Environment (DoE) (1977), *Policy for the Inner City*, Cmnd 6845 (London: HMSO).

Department of the Environment (DoE) (1979), *National Dwelling and Housing Survey, 1977/8* (London: HMSO).

Dex, Shirley (1978–9), 'Job search methods and ethnic discrimination', *New Community*, vol. 7, no. 1 (Winter).

Driver, G. (1977), 'Cultural competence, social power and school achievement: a case study of West Indian pupils attending a secondary school in the West Midlands', *New Community*, vol. 5, no. 4 (Spring/Summer).

Driver, G. (1979), 'Classroom stress and school achievement. West Indian adolescents and their teachers', in V. S. Khan (ed.), *Minority Families in Britain* (London: Macmillan).

Driver, G. (1980), *Beyond Underachievement* (London: Commission for Racial Equality).

Durkheim, Emile (1950), *Suicide* (London: Routledge & Kegan Paul).

Edwards, J. and Batley, R. (1978), *The Politics of Positive Discrimination* (London: Tavistock).

Eisenstadt, S. N. (1956), *From Generation to Generation* (Glencoe, Ill.: The Free Press).

Eysenck, Hans (1971), *Race, Intelligence and Education* (London: Temple Smith).

Fanon, F. (1967), *Black Skin White Masks* (Harmondsworth: Penguin).

Fisher, Sir Henry (1977), *Report of an Inquiry by the Hon. Henry Fisher into the Circumstances leading to the Trial of Three Persons on Charges Arising Out of the Death of Maxwell Confait and the Fire at 27 Doggett Road, S.E. 26* (The Confait Case) (London: HMSO).

Fogelman, Ken (1976) *Britain's Sixteen Year Olds* (National Children's Bureau).

Foner, N. (1979), *Jamaica Farewell: Jamaican Migrants in London* (London: Routledge & Kegan Paul).

Foster-Carter, Olivia (forthcoming), 'Black objects: the black as subject in social science', in Charles Husband (ed.), *Social Psychology and Ethnic Relations* (London: Academic Press).

Freeman, Simon (1979), 'A glimpse of the good life', *Sunday Times*, 25 November.

Fuller, M. (1978), Dimensions of gender in a school, unpublished PhD thesis, University of Bristol.

Gardiner, Lord (1978), quoted in 'A suspicion of injustice', *Guardian*, 30 December.

Garvey, Marcus (1967), *Philosophy and Opinions*, 3 vols (London: Cass).

Genovese, Eugene (1971), *In Black and Red* (London: Allen Lane).

Giles, Raymond (1977), *The West Indian Experience in British Schools* (London: Heinemann).

Hall, Stuart (1980), 'Race, articulation and societies structured in dominance', in Marion O'Callaghan (ed.), *Sociological Theories: Race and Colonialism* (Paris: UNESCO).

Hall, Stuart and Jefferson, Tony (eds) (1976), *Resistance through Rituals*, (London: Hutchinson).

Hall, Stuart, Critcher, Chas., Jefferson, Tony, Clarke, John and Roberts, Brian (1978), *Policing the Crisis: Mugging, the State and Law and Order* (London: Macmillan).

Halsbury's Laws of England (1969), 3rd edn (London: Butterworths).

Hargreaves, D. (1967), *Social Relations in a Secondary School* (London: Routledge & Kegan Paul).

Harris, T. (1971), 'Survey of immigrants in approved schools', unpublished paper, DHSS.

Hebdige, Dick (1979), *Subculture: The Meaning of Style* (London: Methuen).

Heinemann, B. (1972), *The Politics of the Powerless* (London: Oxford University Press for the Institute of Race Relations).

Hill, Clifford (1971), 'Pentecostalist growth – result of racialism?', *Race Today*, vol. 3.

Holdaway, Simon (ed.) (1979), *The British Police* (London: Edward Arnold).

Home Affairs Committee of the House of Commons, Session 1979–80 (1980), *Race Relations and the 'Sus' Law* (London: HMSO).

Home Office (1965), *Immigration from the Commonwealth*, Cmnd 2739 (London: HMSO).

Home Office (1978), *Proposals for Replacing Section 11 of the Local Government Act, 1966*, Consultative Document (London: Home Office).

Home Office (1979), *Evidence to the Royal Commission on Criminal Procedure, Memorandum X* (London: Home Office).

House of Commons (1976–7), 180–1, *Report of the Select Committee on Race Relations and Immigration. The West Indian Community* (London: HMSO).

House of Commons (1979–80), 610–ii, *Memorandum of Evidence from the Home Office to Home Affairs Select Committee* (London: HMSO).

House of Commons (1979–80), 610–iii, *Memorandum of Evidence from the Department of Employment to the Home Affairs Select Committee* (London: HMSO).

House of Commons (1979–80), 610–iv, *Memorandum of Evidence from the Manpower Services Commission to the Home Affairs Select Committee* (London: HMSO).

House of Commons (1979–80), 610–v, *Memorandum of Evidence from the Department of Education and Science to the Home Affairs Select Committee* (London: HMSO).

House of Commons (1979–80, 610–vi, *Memorandum of Evidence from the Department of the Environment to the Home Affairs Select Committee* (London: HMSO).

House of Commons (1979–80, 610–vii, *Memorandum of Evidence from the Commission for Racial Equality to the Home Affairs Select Committee* (London: HMSO).

Humphry, Derek (1972), *Police Power and Black People* (London: Panther).

Hunt, J. (1967), *Immigrants and the Youth Service* (London: HMSO).

Institute of Race Relations (IRR) (1979), *Police against Black People* (London: IRR).

James, D. (1979), 'Police–black relations: the professional solution', in S. Holdaway (ed.), *The British Police* (London: Edward Arnold).

Jardine, Jim (1979), 'Get tough with terrorists', *Police*, vol. 12, no. 2 (October).

Jeffcoate, Robert (1979), *Positive Image* (London: Chameleon Press).

Jefferson, Tony, Critcher, Chas., Hall, Stuart, Roberts, Brian and Clarke, John (1975), *Mugging and Law 'n' Order* (Birmingham University Centre for Contemporary Cultural Studies Occasional Paper, no. 35).

John, G. (1980), *Projects versus Politics: A Report on the Political Cultures of Youth and Community Work with Black People in British Cities* (London: National Association of Youth Clubs).

Johnson, M., Cross, M. and Parker, R. (1981), 'Ethnic minorities and the inner city', unpublished paper presented to the Institute of British Geographers' annual conference.

Jones, Marsha (1980), 'Sugar and spice and all things nice?', *Youth in Society*, no. 39 (February).

Kallynder, Royston and Dalrymple, Henderson (1974), *Reggae: A People's Music* (London: Carib-Arawak).

Kettle, Martin (1981), 'Controlling the police', *New Society*, 8 January.

Khan, Verity Saifullah (ed.) (1979), *Minority Families in Britain: Support and Stress* (London: Macmillan).

Kuhn, A. and Wolpe, A. M. (eds), (1978), *Feminism and Materialism* (London: Routledge & Kegan Paul).

Lacey, Colin (1970), *Hightown Grammar* (Manchester: Manchester University Press).

Ladner, J. (1971), *Tomorrow's Tomorrow: The Black Woman* (Garden City, NY: Doubleday).

Lambert, A. (1976), 'The Sisterhood', in M. Hammersley and P. Woods (eds), *The Process of Schooling* (London: Routledge & Kegan Paul).

Lambert, John (1970), *Crime Police and Race Relations* (London: Oxford University Press for the Institute of Race Relations).

Landes, R. (1955), 'Biracialism in American society', *American Anthropologist*, vol. 57.

Law Centres Federation (LCF) (1979), *Evidence to the Royal Commission on Criminal Procedure: Appendix* (London: LCF).

Lawrence, Daniel (1974), *Black Migrants, White Natives* (London: Cambridge University Press).

Lee, G. and Wrench, J. (1981), *In Search of a Skill* (London: Commission for Racial Equality).

Legal Action Group Bulletin (1981), 'Press reactions to the report' (February).

Leggett, John C. (1968), *Class, Race and Labour* (London: Oxford University Press).

Leigh, L. H. (1975), *Police Powers in England and Wales* (London: Butterworths).

Little, Alan (1975), 'The background of under-achievement in immigrant children in London', in G. K. Verma and C. Bagley (eds), *Race and Education across Cultures* (London: Heinemann).

Llewellyn, Mandy (1980), 'Studying girls at school: the implications of confusion', in R. Deem (ed.), *Schooling for Women's Work* (London: Routledge & Kegan Paul).

Lowenthal, D. (1972), *West Indian Societies* (London: Oxford University Press).

McEachern, J. (1980), 'Shock fall in "sus" arrests', *Daily Mirror*, 18 February.

McConville, M. and Baldwin, J. (1981), 'Justice in danger?', *New Society*, 30 April.

Macdonald, M. (1980), 'Socio-cultural reproduction and women's education', in R. Deem (ed.), *Schooling for Women's Work* (London: Routledge & Kegan Paul).

McNee, Sir David (1980), quoted in '"Sus" not being used to harass blacks, says McNee', *Guardian*, 22 February.

McRobbie, Angela and Garber, Jenny (1976), 'Girls and sub-culture', in S. Hall and T. Jefferson (eds), *Resistance through Rituals* (London: Hutchinson).

Mack, Joanna (1977), 'West Indians and school', *New Society*, 8 December.

Mackie, Lindsay (1978), 'Race and crime research runs into snags', *Guardian*, 18 September.

Mackie, Lindsay (1980), 'Government warned by MPs to repeal "sus" laws', *Guardian*, 7 August.

Makeham, P. (1980), 'The anatomy of youth unemployment', *Department of Employment Gazette*, vol. 88, no. 3.

Manpower Services Commission (MSC) (1977), *Young People and Work* (Holland Report) (London: MSC).

Manpower Services Commission (MSC) (1978), 'Two new programmes to fight unemployment', press notice, 28 February.

Manpower Services Commission (MSC) (1979), *Special Programme, Special Needs* (London: MSC).

Manpower Services Commission (MSC) (1980), *Review of the Second Year of Special Programmes* (London: MSC).

Marsh, Alan (1976), 'Who hates the blacks?', *New Society*, 23 September.

Miles, Robert (1978), *Between Two Cultures? The Case of Rastafarianism*, Working Paper on Ethnic Relations no. 10 (Bristol: SSRC Research Unit on Ethnic Relations).

Miles, Robert and Phizacklea, Annie (1977), 'Class, race, ethnicity and political action', *Political Studies*, vol. 27.

Milner, David (1975), *Children and Race* (Harmondsworth: Penguin).

Mitchell, J. (1975), *Psychoanalysis and Feminism* (London: Allen Lane).

Moore, Robert (1975), *Racism and Black Resistance* (London: Pluto Press).

Muchlinsky, P. T. (1980), 'Arrests and detention', *Human Rights Review*, vol. 5, no. 3 (Autumn).

Mungham, Geoff and Pearson, Geoff (eds) (1976), *Working Class Youth Culture* (London: Routledge & Kegan Paul).

Murdock, Graham (1975), 'Education, culture and the myth of classlessness', in J. T. Haworth and M. A. Smith (eds), *Work and Leisure* (London: Lepus Books).

Murdock, Graham and McCron, Robin (1976), 'Youth and class: the career of a confusion', in G. Mungham and G. Pearson (eds), *Working Class Youth Culture* (London: Routledge & Kegan Paul).

Nairn, Tom (1968), 'Why it happened', in A. Quattrochi and T. Nairn (eds), *The Beginning of the End* (London: Panther).

National Council for Civil Liberties (NCCL) (1975), *Vagrancy: An Archaic Law* (London: NCCL).

National Youth Bureau (NYB) (1979), *Young People and the Police* (Leicester: NYB).

Nuttall, Jeff (1970), 'Techniques of separation', in Tony Cash (ed.), *Anatomy of Pop* (London: BBC Publications).

Oral History and Black History (1980), 'Conference report', *Journal of Oral History*, vol. 8, no. 1 (Spring).

Organisation of Women of Asian and African Descent (1979), 'A dream deferred', *Fowaad*.

Pahl, Jan (1980), 'Patterns of money management within marriage', *Journal of Social Policy*, vol. 9, pt. 3 (July).

Parker, Howard (1974), *View from the Boys: A Sociology of Down-Town Adolescents* (Newton Abbot: David & Charles).

Parkin, Frank (1979), *Marxism and Class Analysis: A Bourgeois Critique* (London: Tavistock).

Parsons, Talcott (1949), *Essays in Sociological Theory* (Glencoe, Ill.: The Free Press).

Parsons, Talcott (1952), *The Social System* (London: Tavistock).

Parsons, Talcott (1961), 'The school class as a social system', in A. H. Halsey, J. Floud and C. Arnold Anderson (eds), *Education, Economy and Society* (Glencoe, Ill.: The Free Press).

Pearson, David G. (1977), 'West Indian Communal Associations in Britain: some observations', *New Community*, vol. 5, no. 4 (Spring/Summer).

Pearson, Geoff (1976), '"Paki-bashing" in a north east Lancashire cotton town: a case study and its history', in Geoff Mungham and Geoff Pearson (eds), *Working Class Youth Culture* (London: Routledge & Kegan Paul).

Phillips, Melanie (1976), 'Brixton and crime', *New Society*, 8 July.

Phizacklea, Annie and Miles, Robert (1980), *Labour and Racism* (London: Routledge & Kegan Paul).

Plowden Report (1967), *Children in Their Primary Schools* (London: HMSO).

Police (1981), 'A code for the police and a charter for the citizen', vol. 12, no. 6 (February).

Pound, J. (1971), *Poverty and Vagrancy in Tudor England* (London: Longman).

Prescod-Roberts, M. (1980), 'Bringing it all back home', in M. Prescod-Roberts and N. Steele (eds), *Black Women: Bringing It All Back Home* (Bristol: Falling Wall Press). .

Prescod-Roberts, M. and Steele, N. (eds) (1980), *Black Women: Bringing It All Back Home* (Bristol: Falling Wall Press).

Pryce, Ken (1979), *Endless Pressure* (Harmondsworth: Penguin).

Pulle, S. (1973), *Police/Immigrant Relations in Ealing* (London: Runnymede Trust).

Rees, T., Stevens, P. and Willis, C. F. (1979), 'Race, crime and arrests', *Home Office Research Bulletin*, no. 8 (London: Home Office).

Rex, John (1980), 'Black power or just another brick in the wall', *The Times Higher Educational Supplement*, 20 June.

Rex, J. and Moore, R. (1967), *Race, Community and Conflict* (London: Routledge & Kegan Paul).

Rex, John and Tomlinson, Sally (1979), *Colonial Immigrants in an English City* (London: Routledge & Kegan Paul).

Robins, David and Cohen, Philip (1978), *Knuckle Sandwich: Growing Up in the Working-Class City* (Harmondsworth: Penguin).

Rosaldo, M. Z. and Lamphere, L. (eds) (1974), *Woman, Culture and Society* (Stanford, Calif.: Stanford University Press).

Rowbotham, Sheila (1973), *Women's Consciousness, Man's World* (Harmondsworth: Pelican).

Rowntree, John and Rowntree, Margaret (1968), 'Youth as a class', *International Socialist Journal*, no. 25 (February).

Royal Commission on Criminal Procedure (1981), *Report*, Cmnd 8092 (London: HMSO).

Scaffardi, S. (1980), '"Sus": lessons of the thirties', *Guardian*, 25 February.

Schulten, P. (ed.) (1981), *Religious Movements* (The Hague: Nijhoff).

Scrap Sus Campaign (1979), *A Fair Deal for All* (London: SSC).

Select Committee on Race Relations and Immigration (1971–2), *Police/Immigrant Relations*, Vol. 1 (London: HMSO).

Select Committee on Race Relations and Immigration (1976–7), Vol. 1 (London: HMSO).

Shanin, Teodor (1978), 'The peasants are coming: migrants who labour, peasants who travel and Marxists who write', *Race and Class*, vol. 19, no. 3 (Winter).

Sharpe, Sue (1976), *Just Like a Girl: How Girls Learn to Be Women* (Harmondsworth: Penguin).

Shaw, J. (1980), 'Education and the individual: schooling for girls, or mixed schooling – a mixed blessing?', in R. Deem (ed.), *Schooling for Women's Work* (London: Routledge & Kegan Paul).

Short, C. (1978), *Talking Blues* (Birmingham: All Faiths for One Race).

Simpson, George Eaton (1955a), 'Political cultism in West Kingston, Jamaica', *Social and Economic Studies*, vol. 4, no. 2 (June).

Simpson, George Eaton (1955b), 'Culture change and reintegration found in the cults of West Kingston, Jamaica', *Proceedings of the American Philosophical Society*, vol. 99, no. 2 (April).

Simpson, George Eaton (1962), 'The Ras Tafari Movement in Jamaica in its millennial aspect', in S. Thrupp (ed), *Millennial Dreams in Action* (The Hague: Mouton).

Smith, David J. (1977), *Racial Disadvantage in Britain* (Harmondsworth: Penguin).

Smith, D. (1980), 'Unemployment and racial minority groups', *Department of Employment Gazette*, vol. 88, no. 6.

Smith, M. G., Augier, Roy and Nettleford, Rex (1967), 'The Ras Tafari movement in Kingston, Jamaica', *Caribbean Quarterly*, vol. 13, nos 3 and 4.

Smith, R. T. (1956), *The Negro Family in British Guiana* (London: Routledge & Kegan Paul).

State Research Bulletin (1979), vol. 2, no. 13 (August–September).

State Research Bulletin (1980), vol. 3, no. 16 (February–March).

State Research Bulletin (1981), vol. 4, no. 22 (February–March).

Stevens, P. and Willis, C. F. (1979), *Race, Crime and Arrests*, Home Office Research Study no. 58 (London: HMSO).

Stevenson, Dennis and Wallis, Peter (1970), 'Second generation West Indians: a study in alienation', *Race Today*, vol. 2, no. 8 (August).

Tanner, N. (1974), 'Matrifocality', in M. Z. Rosaldo and L. Lamphere (eds), *Woman, Culture and Society* (Stanford, Calif.: Stanford University Press).

Taylor, J. H. (1973), 'Newcastle-upon-Tyne: Asian pupils do better than whites', *British Journal of Sociology*, vol. 24, no. 4.

Thomas-Hope, Elizabeth (1980), 'Hopes and reality in the West Indian migration to Britain', *Journal of Oral History*, vol. 8, no. 1 (Spring).

Thrupp, S. (ed.) (1962), *Millennial Dreams in Action* (The Hague: Mouton).

Tierney, John (1980), 'Political deviance: a critical commentary on a case study', *Sociological Review*, vol. 28, no. 4 (November).

Time Out (1981), 'The community may survive this kind of policing', 17–23 April.

Tomlinson, S. (1980), 'West Indian school performance', unpublished paper presented to Conference on Race, Class and the State (University of Sussex).

Troyna, Barry (1977*a*), 'The reggae war', *New Society*, 10 March. Reprinted in *Race and Immigration*, 2nd edn, a New Society Social Studies Reader (London: International Publishing Corporation).

Troyna, Barry (1977*b*), 'Angry youngsters: a response to racism in Britain', *Youth in Society*, no. 26 (June).

Troyna, Barry (1978*a*), 'Race and streaming: a case study', *Educational Review*, vol. 30, no. 1.

Troyna, Barry (1978*b*), 'The significance of reggae music in the lives of black adolescent boys in Britain: an exploratory study', unpublished M. Phil. thesis, University of Leicester.

Troyna, Barry (1978*c*), *Rastafarianism, Reggae and Racism* (Derby: National Association for Multiracial Education).

Troyna, Barry (1979), 'Differential commitment to ethnic identity by black youths in Britain', *New Community*, vol. 7, no. 3 (Winter).

Troyna, Barry (1981), *Public Awareness and the Media: A Study of Reporting on Race* (London: Commission for Racial Equality).

Verma, Gajendra and Bagley, Christopher (1975), *Race and Education across Cultures* (London: Heinemann).

Watson, James L. (ed.) (1977), *Between Two Cultures* (Oxford: Blackwell).

Webb, A. (1980), 'Speech to the research workshop on the transition from school to work', University of Birmingham, 16 December.

Werbner, Prina (1980), 'Rich man, poor man – or a community of suffering', *Journal of Oral History*, vol. 8, no. 1 (Spring).

Werthman, C. (1971), 'Delinquents in school', in B. R. Cosin *et al.* (eds), *School and Society* (London: Routledge & Kegan Paul).

Westergaard, John and Resler, Henrietta (1975), *Class in a Capitalist Society: A Study of Britain* (London: Heinemann).

Whitaker, Ben (1979), *The Police in Society* (London: Eyre Methuen).

Wilkinson, D. (1975), 'Black youth', in R. Havighurst and P. Dreyer (eds), *Youth* (Chicago, Ill.: University of Chicago Press).

Williamson, H. (1980), 'Client responses to the Youth Opportunities Programme', unpublished paper, University of Wales.

Willis, Paul (1977), *Learning to Labour: How Working Class Kids Get Working Class Jobs* (Farnborough, Hants: Saxon House).

Wood, Lisa (1980), 'Young, unemployed . . . and black', *Financial Times*, 13 January.

Working Party on Community/Police Relations in Lambeth (1981), *Final Report* (London: Borough of Lambeth).

Working Party on Vagrancy and Street Offences (Home Office) (1974),
Working Paper (London: HMSO).
Working Party on Vagrancy and Street Offences (Home Office) (1976),
Report (London: HMSO).
Youth Service Information Centre (YSIC) (1972), *Youth Service Provision for Young Immigrants* (Leicester: YSIC).
Zander, Michael (1981a), 'Royal Commission: no grounds for suspicion',
Guardian, 12 January.
Zander, Michael (1981b), 'The fears of the loudest critics seem exaggerated', *Guardian*, 28 January.

Index